Grottasǫngr

THE SONG OF GROTTI

edited by

Clive Tolley

VIKING SOCIETY FOR NORTHERN RESEARCH
UNIVERSITY COLLEGE LONDON
2008

First published 2008

Viking Society for Northern Research, London

ISBN 978-0-903521-78-9

The printing of this book is made possible by a gift
to the University of Cambridge in memory of Dorothea Coke, Skjaeret, 1951.

Typeset in Ehrhardt by Word and Page, Chester, UK

Printed in Great Britain by
Short Run Press Limited, Exeter

Preface

The present edition of *Grottasǫngr* was originally to be included in the fourth volume of *The Poetic Edda*, edited by Ursula Dronke, with the assistance of the present editor, for Oxford University Press. As work progressed on that volume, however, it became clear that a somewhat different and shorter treatment would be needed for this poem, which is not, indeed, found in the Codex Regius which forms the basis of Ursula Dronke's edition. Hence we decided it would be better to issue the present version separately. It is with great pleasure that I am able to offer it for publication through the Viking Society, which does so much to promote scholarship devoted to medieval Scandinavia.

The present edition began as a collaborative effort between me and Ursula Dronke, and reflects many of her suggestions (in particular in the reading of the text itself), though the bulk of the editorial work was carried out by me. The edition was largely already completed before the appearance of the third volume of the edition with commentary by Klaus von See et al., *Kommentar zu den Liedern der Edda* (Heidelberg: Carl Winter, 2000). There is, needless to say, much agreement between them, though the presentation of the material differs. I have not felt it would make a marked improvement to my own edition to repeat the many additional bibliographical references and smaller points of discussion included in the German edition, where they can readily be consulted; von See has aimed at a commendable degree of comprehensiveness in the 128 large pages devoted to the poem, but the present, rather shorter, edition seeks, in the tradition and indeed format set by Ursula Dronke in her own edition of *The Poetic Edda*, to be somewhat more selective and more focused on the presentation of the poem as a literary artefact (though historical and other aspects are not ignored). In keeping with those found in *The Poetic Edda*, the translation aspires to some small degree of poetic expression through the use of alliteration and choice of vocabulary, rather than being purely literal. *Grottasǫngr* is perhaps not among the greatest of works of the ancient North, but it is not without its own interest and attraction, and it is my hope that students and other interested readers will gain some pleasure from investigating the poem through the present edition.

I would like to thank Ursula Dronke for her friendly support (spread over many years, indeed), in particular in the editing of the poem and in bringing this edition to fruition, and Alison Finlay for furthering its publication by the Viking Society. I am also most grateful for the extensive and helpful comments made by my reader, John McKinnell, which have highlighted many points in need of elucidation. Finally, I thank the Dorothea Coke Memorial Fund for providing the necessary financial backing for the publication of this edition.

Clive Tolley
Chester, July 2007

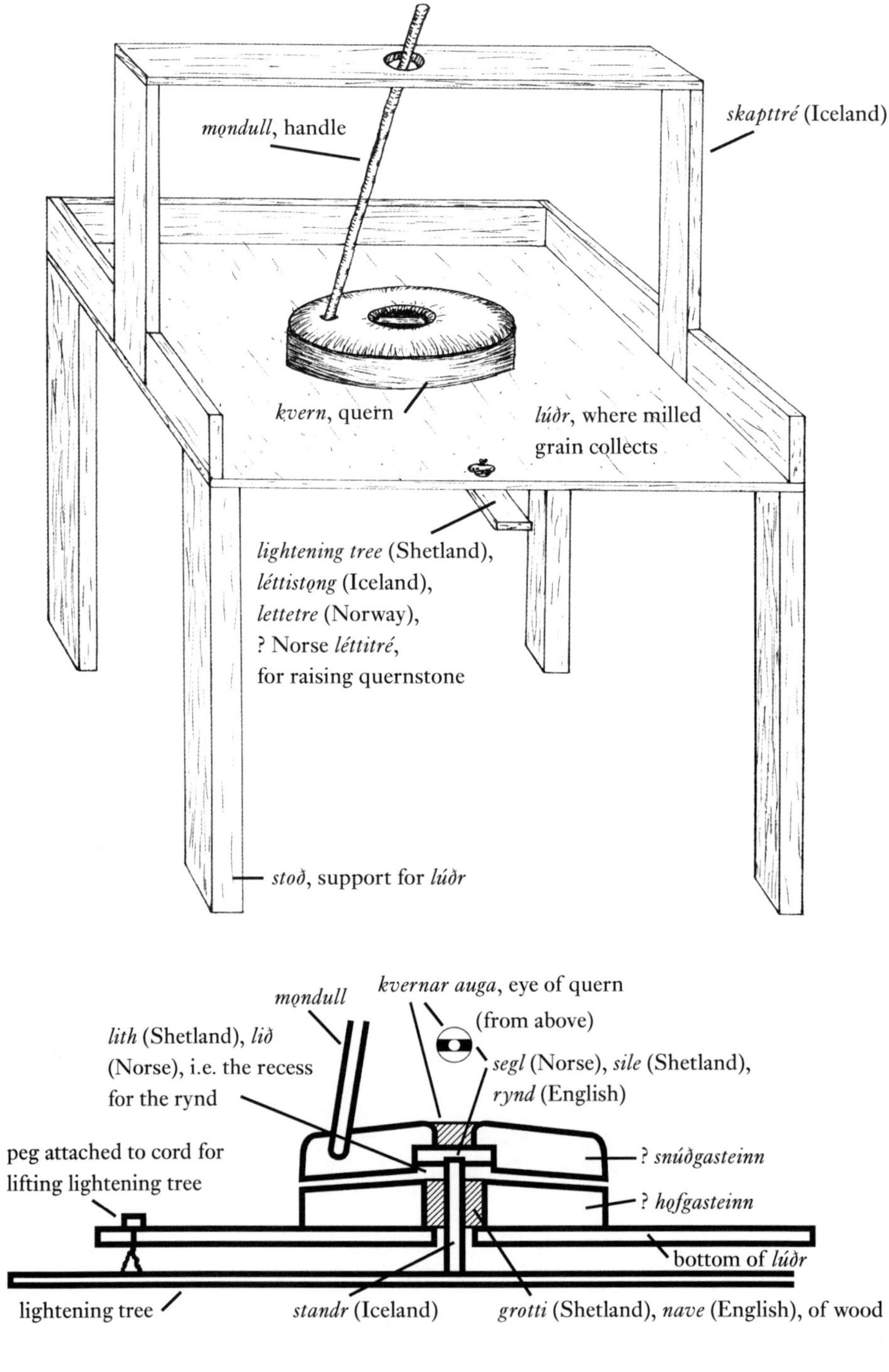

mǫndull, handle

skapttré (Iceland)

kvern, quern

lúðr, where milled grain collects

lightening tree (Shetland), *léttistǫng* (Iceland), *lettetre* (Norway), ? Norse *léttitré*, for raising quernstone

stoð, support for *lúðr*

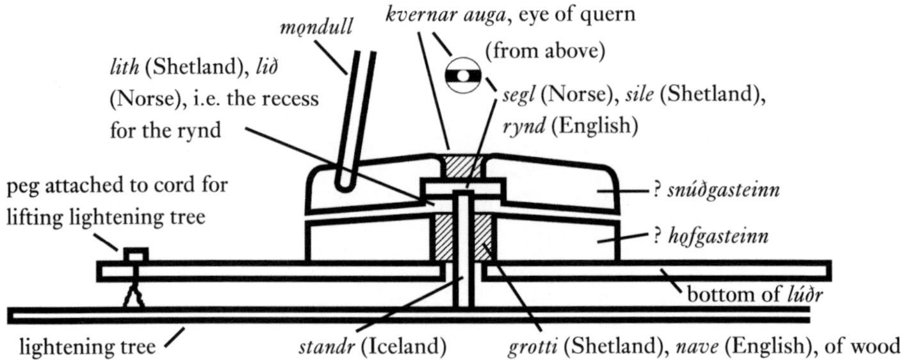

The Norse quern, based on Norwegian, Icelandic and Shetland models.

Introduction

I. *The manuscripts*

Grottasǫngr is preserved in three manuscripts of Snorri's *Edda*, in its entirety in SR and T, and the first stanza alone in C. SR (Codex Regius 2367 4to, formerly in the Royal Library, Copenhagen, now in the Stofnun Árna Magnússonar í íslenskum fræðum, Reykjavík) is from *c*. 1325. It is the primary manuscript source for the present edition of *Grottasǫngr*. T (Codex Trajectinus 1374, in the University Library, Utrecht) is a sixteenth-century copy of a late-thirteenth-century original (*SnE* vii). It is closely related to SR, but is not a copy of it; it is likely that SR and the antecedent of T are copied from one original. This is confirmed in the text of *Grottasǫngr* found in the two manuscripts. That original was itself corrupt in various passages; problematic sections of the poem in SR are not resolved by T. The orthography of T is basically more archaic than that of SR, for example in the use of unstressed 'o' rather than 'u', or the form 'oro' for *voru*, or 'it' for *þit*: some caution is necessary, however: a form such as 'hendor' must be an invention of the T copyist. In two places T omits lines preserved in SR (3/1–2, 18/3), and mistakes, marked for correction, are fairly frequent. Nonetheless, in several instances T has readings preferable to those of SR (e.g. 6/5, 17/5, 18/6, 21/7). The immediate antecedent of T would probably have been more accurate than is SR, but the danger that forms in T itself stem from the sixteenth-century scribe cannot be ignored. T, though valuable, does not preserve the text in a sufficiently good state to supplant SR as the basis for the text of a modern edition. C (AM 748 II 4to, now in the Stofnun Árna Magnússonar í íslenskum fræðum, st. 1 only) dates from *c*. 1400 (*SnE* xiii). In the one stanza cited, the text differs in two points from SR/T: C has *eru* for *erum*, and *giǫrvar* for *hafðar*. The first difference may derive from a desire to avoid the complication of presenting a speech within such a short citation; it may also represent a different textual tradition, as seems to be the case with the second difference (*giǫrvar* and *hafðar* may, however, derive from one (perhaps somewhat corrupt) original written form: this implies that several stages of transmission took place, presumably in the period *c.* 1200–1300, before the extant manuscripts were written). In both cases the SR/T reading seems slightly preferable. It seems unlikely that Snorri intended to quote the whole poem: this would be uncharacteristic, and the poem is not wholly consistent with its prose context. Therefore C may well represent Snorri's original intention, with just the beginning of the poem cited (*SnE* xxii). The differences observed in this one stanza are sufficient warning that the text of the poem known to Snorri may have differed considerably from that preserved in SR/T, where its presence is likely to be due to an early interpolator.

Further discussion of the manuscripts of Snorri's *Edda* is to be found in Faulkes's edition of *Gylfaginning*, xxix–xxxi.

II. *The Norse quern*

At the heart of *Grottasǫngr* lies the ancient Norse hand mill. The form of quern in use in medieval Scandinavia may be ascertained reasonably accurately by examining both archaeological examples, and working querns in use in Norse areas (including Norse areas of Scotland) until recently (see Eiríkr Magnússon 1910; Curwen 1937; *KLNM*, *s.v. kvarn*).

The quernstones rested on a platform or crib (*lúðr*) some feet off the ground, in which the flour would collect. In some querns the upper stone could be adjusted up and down to achieve the best grind with a lightening tree fixed beneath the *lúðr*. In later Icelandic querns the handle rose up to a frame (a ⊓-shaped structure rising from the *lúðr*); the *skapttré* of the poem is best understood as referring to some such device. It is clear from the poem that both the girls are involved in turning the quern; this could imply a quern with two handles, such as were sometimes to be found in parts of Scotland, but it is more likely to indicate that the quern was simply so massive that both had to turn the (one) handle together. Although specific names for the upper and lower stones do not appear to be recorded, the poem's *snúðgasteinn* is probably the top, moving stone, while the lower stone may be indicated by *hǫfgasteinn* (or variants). *Grotti* (cf. English 'grind') in Norn and Norwegian dialect refers specifically to the nave of the lower stone, through which the shaft supporting the upper stone passes.

III. *The sequence of ideas in the poem*

Two cycles of human life intertwine in *Grottasǫngr*. The maidens, sprung from mighty giant kin, first played with rocks in the mountains – the very rocks which were to form the quernstone they were later enslaved to – before engaging in battles as valkyrie figures, and involving themselves in the highest military affairs of kings. Suddenly these mighty beings are reduced to menials, churning out riches for another without rest. Their chagrin is ripe for explosion.

Fróði is the monarch who enslaves these girls. His deceit stems from the combination of traditions the poet has employed in his depiction. On the one hand he embodies the character of Fróði the peacegiver, whose reign was marked by its long peace and prosperity, and on the other that of Fróði, originally a king of the Heathobards of the fifth century, who, in most of the Norse accounts, usurped the throne from his brother, and was subsequently overthrown by his avenging nephews (see §§IV and V). This marrying of different legends enables the poet to allude both to the riches and luxury of Fróði's reign, and to its tyranny. His wealth is derived from a merciless exploitation of his mill-workers, not (as we should expect from the traditional king of peace) from the harmony and goodness of his rule.

The poem presents a confrontation between these two different powers, but it also involves a collision between different sorts of wisdom. *Fróði* encompasses the sense 'wise', but also harks back to a more archaic sense 'virile, fecund'.[1] He epitomises the conviction that a prosperous society depends on the wisdom of its rulers, and once his wisdom falters, so too does the wealth and prowess of his realm. It is upon this conceit that the structure of the poem depends. In contrast to the king, the maidens are said to have foresight, are *framvísar*. Fróði did not anticipate the consequences of the lack of wisdom he showed in neglecting to enquire about the nature of the maidens he obtained: he saw only strength, something to bolster his own power. The maidens, however, declare that the finding of the quernstones and their own presence there to work them was no chance, but was known to them all along. Whilst the audience may not be quite convinced by this self-assuring explanation of their capture and subjugation, the girls nonetheless put their conviction to effect, by milling out an avenger to overthrow Fróði, and overturning the wonder-mill. At this point they declare they have milled enough.

1 The poem opens with a declaration by the two protagonists of their identity, their whereabouts, and their essential nature: Fenja and Menja have come to the house of King Fróði, two girls gifted with foresight. The incongruity of their situation – *máttkar meyiar at mani hafðar* – strikes a foreboding note.

2–4 The girls are taken straight to the mill to start working: the king does not even mention rest before hearing the slave-women's tune. They accordingly set to work: the sound of industry rings out, as they adjust the machine, and the king again orders them to work. The milling, accompanied by the girls' singing, continues until Fróði's household is asleep, and the flour begins to emerge.

5–6 Menja speaks: let them grind out wealth and blessings for Fróði, let him sleep in the lap of luxury – that may then be counted good milling. Echoing the stock descriptions of Fróði's peace found in other sources, she arrogates its establishment to the mill's grinding.

7 With scant thanks for this magnanimity, Fróði, far from offering them rest, tells the girls they may sleep for no longer than a cuckoo stops singing, or the time it took him to sing one song.

8–12 Menja in rejoinder undermines Fróði's reputation for wisdom: he was not wise when he bought slave-girls without finding out about their kindred. She mentions a series of giants, and declares the girls are descended from them. Moreover, the quern Grotti would not have emerged from the earth, nor would the maidens be there to grind it, if they had not had foreknowledge of the whole matter. The maidens themselves moved the grindstones from the earth in their play, and sent them rolling to a place (presumably Denmark) where men discovered them.

13–15 The maidens then engaged in battle in Sweden, toppling and upholding kings as they chose.

16–17 With no explanation as to how it happened, the maidens were then brought in captivity and misery to Fróði's courts, where these erstwhile warmongers were ironically reduced to turning the mill, the 'diffuser of war'. This

[1] See, for example, commentary to *Skírnismál* 1/5 in *PE* II.

perception of their ignominy is the turning point of the poem. Menja concludes by saying their hands must rest: she has milled more than her fair share.

17–20 Fenja takes over the song: they will not rest their hands, she says, before Fróði deems that enough milling is done. The irony of her statement is then revealed: it is spear-shafts that hands shall grasp – and here she taunts the sleeping Fróði: wake up, if you wish to hear our songs! An army will arise and burn down the hall in spite of the prince; she sees the fires burning already: Fróði will not keep the seat of Hleiðr. She exhorts her companion to grasp the mill-handle more firmly: they are not sickened by the gore they are grinding out.

21–3 Seeing the approaching fate, they mill all the harder, until the quern breaks to pieces.

24 The maidens conclude with a short statement to Fróði that they have milled for long enough: his fate, for them, is assured.

IV. *The legendary-historical background of Fróði*

For the poet of *Beowulf*, Froda (Old Norse Fróði) was a king of the Heathobards; in so far as he was a historical character he would have been living at some time around the late fifth century. In Norse records another Fróði is also found, a king of Denmark famed for his long reign of peace and prosperity. A glance at the Norse genealogies reveals that from these two Fróðis has proliferated a whole series of legendary Danish kings called Fróði. Fróði the peace-bringer will be considered more fully in the next section of the Introduction.

The family tree of the Danish kings which may be reconstructed from *Beowulf* reveals that the might of the Scyldings was based in part on marriage alliances between small peoples later forgotten in the Scandinavian record:[2]

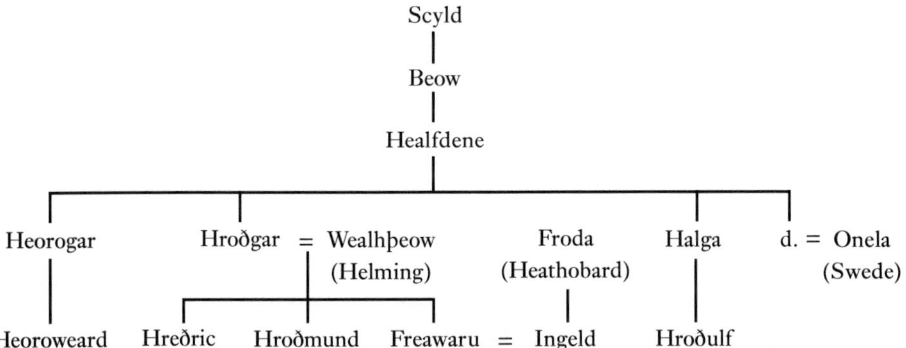

The Heathobards and Danes were enemies. It seems that Froda had slain Healfdene (or Healfdene Froda); some time later Hroðgar attempted to settle the feud by marrying his daughter Freawaru to Froda's son Ingeld. However, as the poet of *Beowulf* forebodes (lines 2032–69), and as *Widsið* says openly (lines 45–9), the Heathobards attacked Heorot, but were defeated. Upon Hroðgar's death,

[2] The manuscript's reading of Beowulf for Beow is widely accepted as a mistaken anticipation of the protagonist's name; I discuss the emendation to Beow in Tolley 1996, 29.

Hroðulf must have seized the throne, slaying Hreðric and Hroðmund. Later, Heoroweard, with a still older claim to the throne, overturned Hroðulf (this much may be gleaned from the Scandinavian sources, though there Hjǫrvarðr's relationship with the royal house is no longer recognised).

The Heathobards have been forgotten as a people by the time of the Norse sources; they are recalled merely in the names Hothbrodus, a Swede in Saxo, and Hǫðbroddr, the enemy of Helgi in the *Helgakviður*. *Hrólfs saga kraka* preserves the closest genealogy to the Old English:[3]

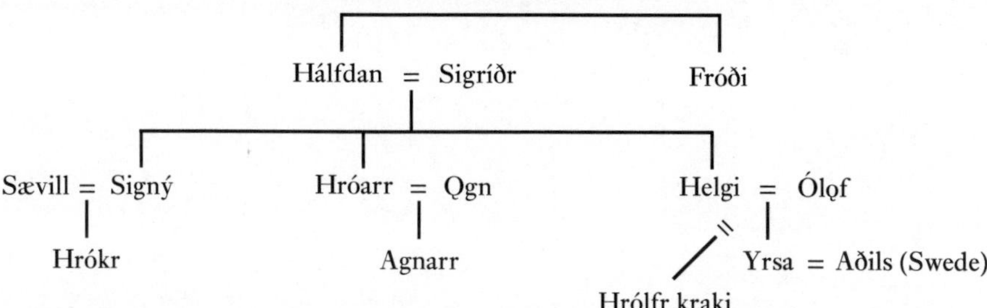

Fróði kills his brother Hálfdan; Hróarr and Helgi take vengeance by burning Fróði in his hall. Helgi is killed by Aðils the Swede. Hróarr is killed by his nephew Hrókr. Hrólfr is killed in an attack by one Hjǫrvarðr, here unrelated.

The genealogy of *Skjǫldunga saga* is given on the next page.[4] The time of Frodo I was one of peace and prosperity (see §V); as an explanation it is stated that Christ was born at this time. Christ's passion was marked by earthquakes and eclipses in Frodo's realm. Frodo was burnt by a criminal named Mysinngus. The death of Frodo III was caused by a deer turning on him and transfixing him with its horns. Frodo IV killed his half-brother Alo; this fratricide is repeated in the next generation, where, after taking vengeance on Sverting for the murder of his father Frodo, Halfdanus is killed by his half-brother Ingialldus, who also takes his widow. Helgo and Roas in turn slay Ingialldus. Roas is then killed by Rærecus and his brother Frodo.

Snorri's genealogy in *Skáldskaparmál*, introducing the story of Grotti, reflects that of *Skjǫldunga saga*:

Óðinn

Skjǫldr Yngvi

Friðleifr

Fróði

[3] *Hrólfs saga* exists in manuscripts from the seventeenth century, based on a lost antecedent of the later sixteenth century (*Hrólfs saga kraka*, ed. Slay, Introduction, xii–xiv), but is believed to have assumed its extant form, itself clearly based on earlier versions of the tale, in the late fourteenth or fifteenth century; elements in the narrative are found earlier, for example in Snorri's *Edda* and *Ynglinga saga*. See Simek and Hermann Pálsson 1987, *s.v. Hrólfs saga kraka*, for further references to discussions of the saga's date and provenance..

[4] *Skjǫldunga saga* is from 1180–1200, but is preserved only in a sixteenth-century Latin summary, *Rerum Danicarum fragmenta*, by Arngrímur Jónsson. The dating is that of Bjarni Guðnason (1963, 315); he notes that Gunnlaugr Leifsson probably knew *Skjǫldunga saga* when he wrote his saga of Óláfr Tryggvason around 1200.

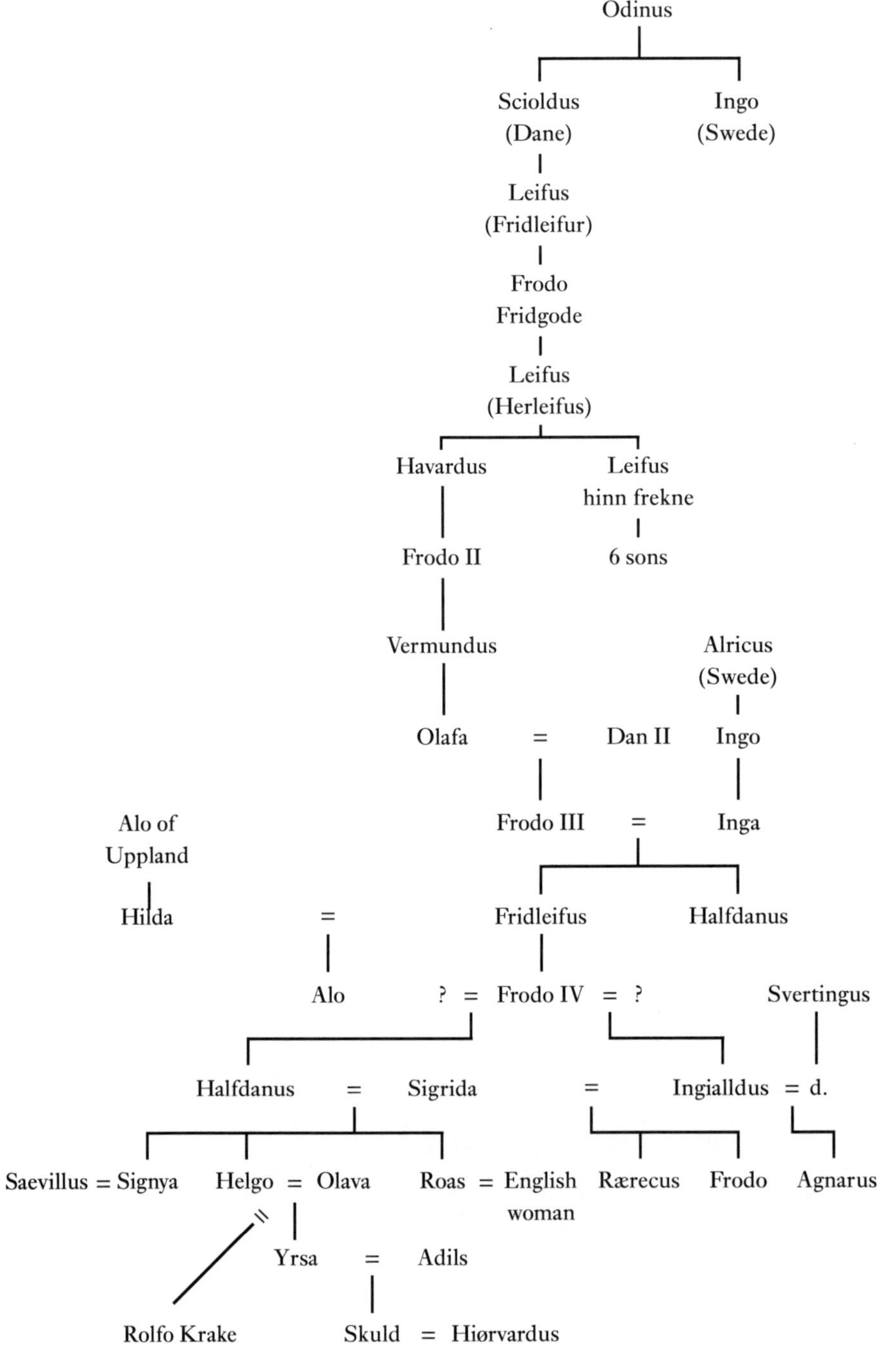

The Danish genealogies of Skjǫldunga saga

Dan
Lother
Skiold
Gram
Hading
Frotho I — Svanhvit = Ragner (Swede)
Haldan — Roe — Skat — Hothbrod
Roe — elf woman = Helgo = Thora — Athisl — Høther
Hiarvarth = Skuld — Yrsa
Rolvo

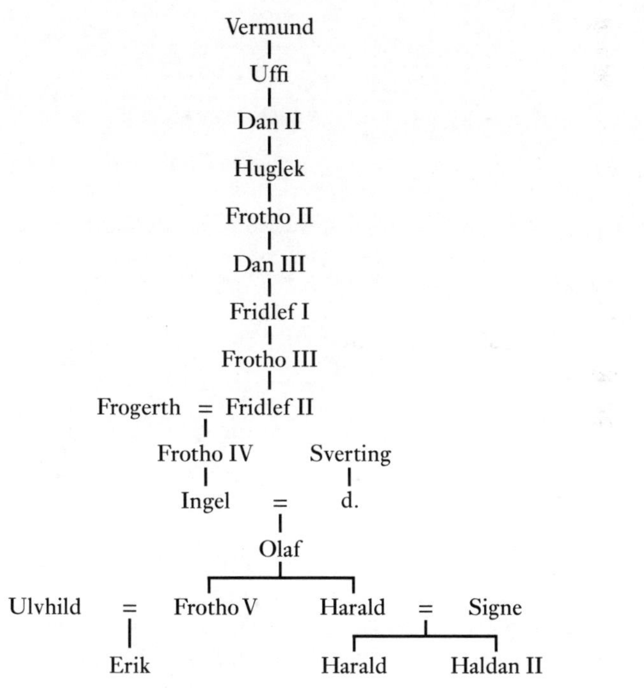

The Danish genealogies of Saxo Grammaticus (selection)

Ynglinga saga (probably by Snorri) also follows *Skjǫldunga saga* (which is explicitly mentioned as a source); the Danish genealogy, in so far as it is given, is identical. Three Fróðis are mentioned: frið-Fróði (ch. 11), on a visit to whom the Swedish king Fjǫlnir drowns in a vat of mead, corresponds to Frodo I of *Skjǫldunga saga*; Fróði inn mikilláti or friðsami (ch. 25) corresponds to Frodo III of *Skjǫldunga saga*; and Fróði inn frœkni (ch. 26), the Frodo IV of *Skjǫldunga saga*.

Snorri's prose setting for *Grottasǫngr*, which is not in agreement with the content of the poem, is derived in part from *Skjǫldunga saga*. Snorri identifies the Fróði of the poem as the first Fróði, of the peace, and makes no connection with the later Fróði (i.e. *Skjǫldunga saga*'s Fróði IV, the original Heathobard). The poem's information that the giant maids fought in Sweden probably prompted Snorri to imagine their acquisition as slaves as taking place on a visit by Fróði to the Swedish Fjǫlnir (kings associated with each other already in *Ynglingatal*). The demise of peace-Fróði is already associated in *Skjǫldunga saga* with Mýsingr, though the latter is not a sea-king there; he is listed as a sea-king in *þulur*, however, and Snorri may have known both the tale of the death of peace-Fróði (Frothi III) in Saxo, where he is gored by a witch transformed into a sea-cow, and the aetiological folktale of the wonder-mill stolen by a sea-captain, which ends up in the ocean grinding salt.

Sven Aggesen (*c.* 1190) has the following genealogy in ch. 1 of his *Brevis historia*:

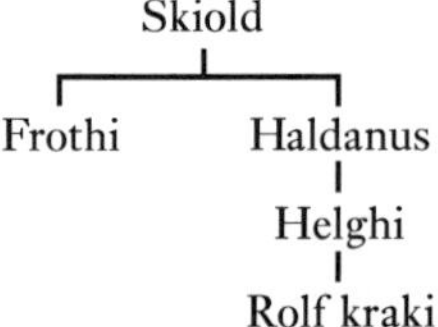

According to Sven, it was Frothi that was killed by Haldanus; he is alone in presenting this reversal of the usual tradition. Sven also mentions Ingeld, but in a lower section of the royal genealogy (ch. 4):

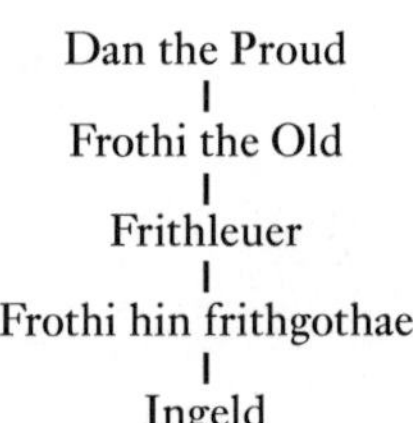

The genealogical elaboration and repetition reaches its climax in Saxo, who presents us with no fewer than five Frothos in the legendary part of his history. The relevant sections of Saxo's Danish genealogy are given on the previous page. Four of these Frothos clearly developed from the original Heathobard king, and from the mythical law-giver (the position of Frotho II, about whom little is said, is unclear). Although Fróði I becomes a Danish king in Norse tradition, and he is dissociated from Ingjaldr, yet the genealogy of *Beowulf* may still be perceived through the later accretions and distortions. Roe is attacked and killed by Hothbrod, whom Helgi in turn slays; this is the reminiscence of the Heathobard Ingeld's attack upon Hroðgar. Haldan kills his two brothers Roe and Skat – something with no counterpart in the Old English.

Saxo uses a source closely resembling *Hrólfs saga kraka* in his history of Frotho V; thus, though the names have changed (apart from Frotho's), the story is essentially a variant of that of Frotho I (whose genealogy is closer to *Hrólfs saga*). Thus Frotho V kills his brother Harald, and is then burnt by Harald's two sons.

Frotho IV with his son Ingel also clearly form a differently remembered version of the story of Froda and Ingeld. Ingel is stirred up by the gruff warrior Starkatherus to take vengeance for his father's death on the family of Sverting, the Saxon (a change resulting from the incorporation of the Heathobards into the Danish family).

Frotho III has the longest treatment of any Frotho in Saxo, taking up the whole of book V of the work. He is regarded as a law-giver and founder of long peace, whose reign coincided with the birth of Christ. He sets up a gold ring at a crossroads to encourage his people to be law-abiding through a fear of the punishment that would follow the theft of the ring. However, a woman incites her son to steal it. She turns herself into a sea-cow and her sons into calves. Frotho arrives in a carriage and stares in amazement at them. She sinks her horn into his flank, killing him. However, his men keep his body embalmed for three years, carrying it around the land in a carriage.

Grottasǫngr is composed in a tradition where Fróði is the son of Friðleifr, as (in various of his manifestations) he is in all the recorded Norse sources except *Hrólfs saga* (which is silent on the matter), although in earlier (pagan) tradition it is unlikely that Friðleifr was considered a father of Fróði (see below). It is likely too that the Fróði of the poem is intended to recall Fróði the fratricide of *Hrólfs saga*; even if st. 22 is rejected as an interpolation, it is this Fróði, rather than peace-Fróði, who is overthrown by a hostile attack such as is ground out by the giant maidens.

It would seem that two traditions stand behind the poem. On the one hand, a legendary history resembling *Hrólfs saga* has been used to inform the picture of the tyrannical king, against whom vengeance is eventually taken; on the other, the depiction of Fróði as the king of peace and wealth derives from a source similar to *Skjǫldunga saga*. Both of these sources were also used by Saxo, and both may be dated to the late twelfth century (though not precisely in their extant forms). The other, later sources considered here represent further elaborations of the traditions concerning Fróði, and do not appear to have been known to the poet of *Grottasǫngr*.

V. *The mythological background*

Three mythological narrative elements may be identified in *Grottasǫngr*: the king, Fróði, renowned for a reign of peace and prosperity; the giantesses who bring about his downfall; and the mill, Grotti, which is the guarantor both of the king's welfare and of his fall. Let us consider them in turn.

King Fróði

The god of fertility and his peace

The time of earthly paradise under the gold-milling Fróði mirrors the early epoch of the gods recounted in *Vǫluspá* 6–8, where they forged gold in plenty, and were happy. The legendary history of Fróði is elevated to the level of myth through this allusion to the theme of a divine age of plenty.

Fróði's golden age is described in several of the sources. Of Frodo I, son of Fridleifur, *Skjǫldunga saga* reports (ch. 3, ÍF 35, 5–6):

> Sed et hujus tempora pax et qvies publica coronabat, ut nullus ne patris qvidem sui interfectorem laedere vel ulcisci fas sibi duceret. Tum etiam vulgo a rapinis et furtis cessatum est, adeo ut in via publica, qvae per tesqva Jalangursheide ducebat, jacentem multis annis anulum aureum, cuivis obvium, nemo tolleret.

> His times were crowned by peace and public quiet, so that no one arrogated to himself the right even to harm or take vengeance on his father's slayer. At that time robbery and theft ceased to such an extent that no one took a gold ring, which lay for many years in full view of everyone beside the highway which led across the wastes of Jalangrsheiðr.

Noting that Christ was born at this time, the account continues:

> Fertur etiam fuisse hoc tempore incredibilis annonae in Dania proventus, apibus eam abundasse, agriqve perhibentur et pascua sponte floruisse, graminaqve (ut ait ille) injussa viruisse, metalla passim in Dania magna copia effossa esse; qvorum artem ipse Rex Frodo probe calluerit.

> It is also said that at this time there was an unbelievable produce of crops in Denmark, that bees were in abundance, the fields and meadows grew spontaneously, and the hay (he says) flourished unbidden, and that metals were mined in great quantities in various places of Denmark; in the craft of metals King Frodo himself was thoroughly versed.

The end of Frodo's reign occurred in this manner:

> Deinde post multorum annorum curriculum insveta facta ecclipsis solis cum terræ motu saxa et scopulos loco movente atqve disrumpente. Illum igitur putant fuisse annum et tempus passionis Christi. Post hæc Frodo rex (a sui temporis pace publica dictus Frode fridgode) authore sceleris qvodam Mysinngo incendio peremptus est.

> Then after the course of many years there occurred an unwonted eclipse of the sun and an earthquake, in which rocks and crags were dislodged and cast down. It is believed that this occurred in the year and at the time of the passion of Christ. After this King Frodo (named Fróði friðgoði after the public peace of his time) was destroyed by fire, a certain Mýsingr being the engineer of the crime.

Related accounts have similar observations: *Upphaf allra frásagna* (along with the Rymbegla collection (AM 730 4to), an eighteenth-century compilation derived from *Skjǫldunga saga*) notes, for example (ÍF 35, 40):

> Á dǫgum Fróða var svá mikill friðr, at engi vildi mann drepa, þó at sæi fyrir sér bundinn fǫðurbana sinn eða bróður.
>
> In Fróði's day there was such great peace that no one wished to kill anyone, even if he saw the slayer of his father or brother bound up in front of him.

Ynglinga saga relates (ch. 10, ÍF 26, 24):

> Á hans [Freys] dǫgum hófsk Fróðafriðr. Þá var ok ár um ǫll lǫnd. Kenndu Svíar þat Frey. [. . .] Freyr hét Yngvi ǫðru nafni. Yngva nafn var lengi síðan haft í hans ætt fyrir tígnarnafn, ok Ynglingar váru síðan kallaðir hans ættmenn.
>
> In Freyr's days arose the Fróði peace. There were good harvests in all lands then; the Swedes attributed this to Freyr. [. . .] Freyr was called by another name, Yngvi. The name Yngvi was thereafter long kept in his family as a title of honour, and his family was thereafter called the Ynglingar.

Snorri's account, closely matching the first citation from *Skjǫldunga saga* above, is given below as part of the prose introduction to the poem.

The account of the peace of Fróði's reign is similar in Saxo (V, xv; here it is Frotho III who is the peace-Fróði); Saxo relates that Frodo abstained from war for thirty years, and turned his attention to establishing homeland security by rooting out theft and robbery. Saxo includes the story of the ring on Jalangrsheiðr (here merely designated 'Jutland'); for Saxo, there was no lack of desire to seize it, but Frodo's terrible authority was so great that no one dared. Saxo then notes that Christ was born at this time, bestowing a sort of peace on the whole world. Saxo is likely to have derived his account from *Skjǫldunga saga*, where the linking of the peace of Augustus (stemming, in Christian understanding, from the birth of Christ at that time) with the peace of Fróði is first likely to have taken place.

The peace of Fróði is witnessed much earlier, however; already around 986 Einarr Helgason mentions in *Vellekla* 18 (*Skj* B I, 120) that no prince had worked such a peace as his present patron except Fróði. The 'golden age' is a widespread folktale motif; the peace of Fróði is the Danish variant of it. The Norse golden age differs markedly from, for example, the classical, where it is a pre-lapsarian time of plenty, unfettered by laws (see Ovid's *Metamorphoses*, book I, 89–112). Saxo's is by far the longest account of the reign of peace-Fróði, and is undoubtedly elaborated from a much simpler core of tradition. Central to his account, however, is that the peace is established through long war, and its maintenance requires a set of detailed laws. Baetke (1942, 39) makes the important point that peace – a condition of political and legal harmony and order where welfare flourishes – was not regarded as a natural condition, but a *donum sacrum* that called for sacrifice.[5]

[5] '*friðr* ist die Gesamtheit jener rechtlich-sittlichen Ordnungen, die ein friedliches und fruchtbares Zusammenleben in der politischen Gemeinschaft gewährleisten. [. . .] Darin, dass die Germanen um den Frieden opferten, spricht sich ihr Glaube aus, dass er nicht eine menschliche Institution oder eine natürliche Ordnung, sondern eine göttliche Stiftung ist, ein donum sacrum, das mittels des Kultes immer wieder auf die Volksgemeinschaft herabgezogen werden muss.'

Fróði is in origin a title, 'the wise/virile'. His particular gifts are seen to be bestowed in an abundance of produce, accompanied by peace, and also in the laws he established. Both elements may be regarded as ancient. He is said to be the son of Friðleifr; this may be a result of later genealogising trends. It is likely that *friðleifr* too was originally a title. The element *-leifr* is common in names, and indicates 'offspring'. The precise purport of *friðleifr* perhaps cannot be determined, but it would appear to emphasise the element of inheritance: Fróði is a 'son of peace', who must hand on the divine gift to his heirs.

To Friðleifr in Norse corresponds, in the Old English genealogies, *Frealaf*, containing the name Frea (i.e. the Norse Freyr). Snorri, in the passage cited above, indicates that while peace reigned in Denmark under Fróði, in Sweden it was attributed to Freyr. In *Skírnismál* 1 Freyr is actually called *inn fróði*. We have here local expressions of the same mythological notion of an age of peace and plenty guaranteed by a semi-divine king. The link between Freyr and Fróði may be traced elsewhere. Snorri says that Freyr was also called by the name Yngvi. Freyr, like Fróði, is in origin a title, and is probably not as ancient as Yngvi, a name which is implied already in Tacitus' name for one of the divisions of the Germani, the Ingvaeones. In Old English Ing was associated in particular with Denmark: he is a demigod who appears among the Danes in the *Rune Poem*, and in *Beowulf* the lord of the Danes is called *frea Ingwina* (de Vries 1956–7, §461). In Saxo book VI the father of Frotho IV is Fridlefus, who marries the Norwegian princess Frogertha; on his way to acquiring her he also has a relationship with a farm-girl Juritha. Behind this surely lies a reminiscence of the wooing of Gerðr by Freyr (told in *Skírnismál*), which has perhaps been split between the two girls in Saxo.

The bringing of *ár ok friðr*, economic and societal well-being, is to be related to the account of Nerthus given by Tacitus in *Germania* ch. 40; Nerthus corresponds phonologically to Njǫrðr in Norse, the father of Freyr:

> Contra Langobardos paucitas nobilitat; plurimis ac valentissimis nationibus cincti non per obsequium sed proeliis et periclitando tuti sunt. Reudigni deinde et Aviones et Anglii et Varini et Eudoses et Suarines et Nuitones fluminibus aut silvis muniuntur. nec quicquam notabile in singulis, nisi quod in commune Nerthum, id est Terram matrem, colunt eamque intervenire rebus hominum, invehi populis arbitrantur. est in insula Oceani castum nemus, dicatumque in eo vehiculum, veste contectum; attingere uni sacerdoti concessum. is adesse penetrali deam intellegit vectamque bubus feminis multa cum veneratione prosequitur. laeti tunc dies, festa loca quaecumque adventu hospitioque dignatur. non bella ineunt, non arma sumunt; clausum omne ferrum; pax et quies tunc tantum nota, tunc tantum amata, donec idem sacerdos satiatam conversatione mortalium deam templo reddat. mox vehiculum et vestis et, si credere velis, numen ipsum secreto lacu abluitur. servi ministrant, quos statim idem lacus haurit; arcanus hinc terror sanctaque ignorantia quid sit illud quod tantum perituri vident.

The Langobardi, in contrast, are famous for being so few; hemmed in by many mighty nations, they obtain safety not through servility but by running the risks of battle. Then come the Reudigni, the Aviones, the Anglii, the Varini, the Eudoses, the Suarines, and the Nuitones, defended by rivers

> or woods. There is nothing noteworthy about them individually, except that collectively they worship Nerthus, or Mother Earth, and believe that she takes part in human affairs and rides among the peoples. On an island in the Ocean is a sacred grove, and in it a consecrated wagon covered with hangings; to one priest alone is it permitted so much as to touch it. He perceives when the goddess is present in her innermost recess, and with great reverence escorts her as she is drawn along by heifers. Then there are days of rejoicing, and holidays are held wherever she deigns to go and be entertained. They do not begin wars, they do not take up arms; everything iron is shut away; peace and tranquillity are only then known and only then loved, until again the priest restores to her temple the goddess, sated with the company of mortals. Then the wagon and hangings and, if you will, the goddess herself are washed clean in a hidden lake. Slaves perform this service, and the lake at once engulfs them: there is as a result a mysterious fear and a sacred ignorance about something seen only by those doomed to die.

The general reliability of Tacitus' account has been called into question; thus, for example, North (1997, 1–25) and von See (1981, 42–72) argue that there was in reality no goddess in this Germanic cult but rather a male god, and that Tacitus was heavily influenced in his depiction by the Terra Mater celebrations in Rome. As a Roman without direct personal familiarity with the area he describes, it is likely that Tacitus' understanding of Germanic practices was distorted in some respects, but the extent of this distortion is a matter of debate; it is impossible to engage in a detailed discussion of this topic here, but the general reliability of Tacitus' account is defended by (among others) McKinnell (2005, 50–2), and this is the approach adopted here.

The annual peace, maintained during the divine visitation, may be seen as a ritual realisation of the formative primordial peace. The *ár ok friðr* of Fróði's reign are a mythological representation of the same primordial peace. There is clearly some geographical continuity from Tacitus' day; although the isle in the ocean cannot be specifically identified, Tacitus' description is precise enough to indicate that one of the Danish islands must be intended. The nearest parallel to Nerthus' perambulation amongst her peoples occurs in the tale of Gunnarr helmingr (in *Ǫgmundar þáttr dytts*), which is set among the Swedes. Gunnarr takes the place of the god Freyr, and makes the attendant girl pregnant – a sign of blessing, in the Swedes' eyes. The two are carted around the country, bringing blessing wherever they come.[6]

There is little extant record of any ritual focused on Fróði. Saxo reports that after he died, Fróði III was carried around the country (under the pretence of being alive), which may be a reflection of an earlier perambulation of the land, such as occurred with Nerthus and Freyr.

[6] It is likely that the Swedes, like the Danes, had an ancient tradition of a time of peace marked in a ritual manner. Tacitus says less about the more distant Suiones (Swedes), but his one piece of information is that all weapons there are kept in the care of a slave; he believes the Swedes, in their remote position, scarcely feared invasion, but it is more likely that a particular period of sacred peace is referred to, such as occurred later in the great gatherings at Uppsala, as reported in the eleventh century by Adam of Bremen in his 'Descriptio insularum aquilonis'.

The emergence from the lake, and return thereto after blessing the land, is to be seen as an enactment of the yearly cycle of the seasons, determined by the waxing and waning power of the sun.

The peace of Fróði is signified in the gold ring left unmolested on Jalangrsheiðr. The ring is associated with various motifs, an important one being oaths, sworn by a god on a ring. The chief association here however is surely with Draupnir, the ring which dripped clones of itself (e.g. *Skírnismál* 21) – an unending source of gold, just like Grotti – and therefore represents fertility. A gold ring is clearly also a symbol of the sun. Although the tale of a ring left in a public place without being touched is a commonplace motif illustrating the great peace achieved by some monarch or other (cf. the drinking bowls left by Edwin of Northumbria beside the highway, which none dared to tamper with: Bede, *Ecclesiastical History* II, 16), the associations of the ring with fertility suggest that it may have been an ancient emblem of Fróði.

The end of the peace-god

In *Grottasǫngr* Fróði meets his end in a hostile attack which burns him in his hall; the perpetrator is not named, but if any reliance at all can be placed on st. 22, the attack appears to be one of revenge arising out of the family affairs of the heroic Fróði, not of frið-Fróði. *Skjǫldunga saga*, however, relates that Fróði was burnt in his hall by a criminal named Mysinngus; possibly the poem once contained the same information before the interpolation of st. 22. Snorri expands the reference to Mýsingr, explaining that he was a sea-king who attacked by night, slew Fróði, and fled with booty and Grotti. Snorri has seen in his sources a connection between Mýsingr and Grotti (whether the source be *Skjǫldunga saga* or an earlier version of *Grottasǫngr*), and knows of Mýsingr as a sea-king (as recorded in the *þulur*); using this information he has attributed to Mýsingr the story of how Grotti ended up in the sea churning out salt (a folk motif which may already have become attached to Grotti).

The name *Mýsingr* is formed from *mús*, 'mouse'. In Near Eastern belief mice are deleterious vermin (Krappe 1936), and similar ideas are recorded in folk belief elsewhere; the fall of other presiders over the age of peace often took place at the hands of some beast – mice, of course, are archetypal grain-nibblers, so Mýsingr appears as a murine destroyer of Fróði, seen as a king whose wealth and fertility depends on grain (here transmuted into gold).

Frodo III, a later successor of peace-Fróði, dies in the following manner in *Skjǫldunga saga* (ch. 7(ii), ÍF 35, 15): *Hic cum cervum venatu assecutus hasta transfoderet, cervi conversi cornibus ventrem et viscera confixus occubuit*, 'After piercing with a spear a stag he had pursued in the hunt, he was transfixed in the stomach and guts by the antlers of the deer as it turned round, and died'. This is similar to the death of peace-Fróði (Frotho III) in Saxo (V, xvi); the gold ring which Frotho had set up on some crossroads as a symbol of his peace was stolen at the instigation of a woman. Frotho descended upon the woman's home, but she turned herself into a sea-cow and her sons into calves. When Frotho climbed out of his carriage, the sea-cow thrust her tusk into his flank, killing him. This shares the motif of the emergence from the sea with the representation of Mýsingr as a sea-king. *Ynglinga saga* ch. 26 tells of the fall of King Egill of Sweden: he contended long with one Tunni, 'tusk', before being killed by the horn of a wild bull. A comparable account is found in *Beowulf*, where the Swedish king Ongenðeow is killed by the brothers Eofor and Wulf, 'boar' and 'wolf'; Ongenðeow corresponds genealogically to the Norse Egill. As a successor to Freyr, the Swedish king was, it would seem, believed to mirror, or re-enact, the illustrious life and death of the dynasty's founder. The death of the fertility god by the horns or teeth of wild animals is matched in Middle Eastern myths, which appear to follow a comparable (if not necessarily directly related) mythological pattern; for example, Adonis was killed by the tooth of a wild bear (de Vries 1956–7, §462).

The aftermath of the fertility god's death is also significant. In *Ynglinga saga* Freyr dies of illness, but his death is concealed from the populace. He is buried in a mound, into which taxes are placed, and the good seasons continue. Only after this has continued for some time do the people learn that he is in fact dead; they then ascribe the continuance of good seasons to Freyr's presence in the realm (even though dead). Saxo tells a similar story about Frotho III; after he has been killed by the sea-cow, he continues to be carried around his realm in his carriage, until the advanced state of his body's decay obliges the officials to reveal that he is dead, whereupon he is buried in a mound. Although this carrying of the dead king about the realm must be linked to the motif of the perambulations of the divinity, in a car, found in the accounts of Nerthus and Freyr (the tale of Gunnarr helmingr), as Schier (1968, 394) points out, there appears no parallel to the carrying around of a dead king. Clearly the Swedes regarded even the dead Freyr as bestowing blessings of fertility on his realm, however; with this may be compared the account of the Norwegian king Hálfdan svarti, whose followers, according to *Heimskringla*, arranged that portions of his body should be buried in the various quarters of his realm to ensure its well-being (ÍF 26, 93). Schier argues that the death of Freyr, and indeed of Fróði, cannot be interpreted as a mythological representation of the ritual of death and rebirth, such as takes place with other fertility gods like Zamolxis, as there is no return from death in the Norse examples. He notes, however, that it may not be the return of the god as such, but his death which effects unfailing fertility; this might be supported by the occurrence of strangely ritualised deaths among many of the Ynglingar, which could be seen as re-enactments of the original fertility-generating royal sacrifice.[7] It is also to be inferred from *Ynglingatal* that the divine gift of good seasons was inherited from the dynastic founder, and hence that founder would not be conceived of as returning personally. As Schier notes (1968, 393), a returning god of fertility would be more likely to generate an annual festival; one whose power is communicated to his descendants might be celebrated on a different time-scale, as was the case with the nine-yearly festival at Uppsala.

[7] The death by sickness of Freyr in *Ynglinga saga* is out of tune with the repeated motif of untimely death caused by an animal found among fertility beings. Saxo's account of Frotho III's death may represent a more archaic pattern, especially given the Norse and Old English accounts of the death of Egill/Ongenðeow (and analogues from elsewhere for this sort of fertility-god death). We may suspect that the most ancient evidence we have, namely *Beowulf*, preserves a hint of the most ancient layer of myth when it names Eofor as the king's slayer. The boar was sacred to Freyr: did the god receive his life-giving death from his own sacred animal?

The giantesses

The narrative argument of the tale of *Grottasǫngr* would, in its neatest form, lead to a conclusion in which the gold-producing mill – and in its wake the king who depends upon it – is destroyed by its giantess workers overstraining themselves in an act of vengeance against a cruel and greedy tyrant. There is no need to involve Danish heroic history, with the invasion and burning of the hall: its presence in the poem has resulted from confusion between the Fróði of the mythological peace, and the Fróði of a later heroic age. This confusion may already have taken place by Eyvindr skáldaspillir's time, however (late tenth century; see p. 25).

The role of the giantesses in the Grotti myth may parallel that of the giant maidens in *Vǫluspá* 8, where they appear to break in on the happy and gold-rich gods as they play with *tǫflur* (presumably in a form of chess-game): the implication is that the giantesses join in the game and, we are to assume, win, which results in the demise of the golden age for the Æsir, represented by the loss of the chequers (they turn up again in the new world in *Vǫluspá* 58, symbolising the new golden age), just as Fróði's loss of Grotti marks his end.[8] In both cases the giantesses are underestimated, and in both they achieve their aim, which from the consequences we must surmise to be to undermine the gold and good fortune, the *ár ok friðr*, of society. Yet in *Grottasǫngr* it is not clear that the giantesses were truly acting with fixed purpose from the beginning, even though in st. 1, 10, 13 they claim some sort of foreknowledge. What we are presented with is a 'fall from grace' in their social position, beginning with their playing with the huge stones like children in their own land, then becoming involved in the sordid politics and wars of men, and finally becoming enslaved to a tyrant. There is no real purpose in this *curriculum vitae*, and it was mere chance that they happened to be responsible for wrenching the great boulders from the mountain side, which later became the raw material of the quern. But looking back from their abject position, and contemplating the momentous events they are about to inaugurate, they impose their own fatalism upon their life story: now, it was not chance that they pulled up those rocks, but their own foreknowledge, which in due course has brought them to this plight, now seen as a deliberate self-humiliation, almost a divine kenosis, to enable them to bring about deliverance from the tyrant Fróði. Even so, it seems that they were not in a position, or indeed willing, to carry out their design without some justification from Fróði's actions, so that they became agents of a destruction which essentially he had brought upon himself. It does not seem that the giantesses have any purpose with regard to the mill itself (such as retrieving it): for them, it had been mountain rocks, playthings which it took men to turn to use. They had no need for such a machine.

The motif of the enslavement of a superhuman being resulting in the undoing of the enslaver is also found in *Vǫlundarkviða*. Vǫlundr is *álfa lióði*, 'lord of elves' (st. 11), dwelling on the very edge of human ken, and is characterised in the prose introduction to the poem as son of the king of the remote *Finnar*, the Sámi, who were stereotypically famed for their wily and deceitful magical

[8] See van Hamel (1934, 220–1), whose interpretation I follow, on the 'golden age' of the gods in *Vǫluspá*.

practices. Like Fenja and Menja, Vǫlundr is forced to produce gold trinkets for the cruel King Níðuðr whilst being held captive, until he works his vengeance and escapes. Yet, despite both poems making use of a similar basic motif, they manipulate their material in quite different ways. Fróði suffers from the aloof arrogance of ignorance: it is below him to bother investigating the family history of his slave girls, and this proves his undoing once he treats them badly. Níðuðr is not ignorant of who Vǫlundr is: rather, he is bent upon control of all around him, both people and wealth, and seeks to lessen Vǫlundr's power sufficiently to keep him captive – but he merely injures him physically, leaving his otherworldly magical skills intact, which enable him to make his final escape and lord it over the defeated Níðuðr as he does so, hovering in the air above. *Vǫlundarkviða* is a far more sophisticated and finely wrought work of art than is *Grottasǫngr* (see the discussions of the poem in *PE* II), and the focus of attention is different: *Grottasǫngr* is concerned to show the dark underbelly of the 'golden age' of the *Fróða friðr*, truly a sham which is bought at the price of inhuman cruelty towards the underclasses, a cruelty which indeed turned initial goodwill into hatred on the part of the giantesses. The author of the poem is moreover concerned with lineage: explicitly so in the case of the giantesses, whose ancestry reveals them to be other than they appear to Fróði, and also by implication in the case of Fróði himself, whose complex family history has been shown above to have been a great source of interest in medieval Scandinavia.

The mill Grotti

The folktale wonder-working mill

Folktale type ATU 565, 'The magic mill', is of widespread occurrence. A Scandinavian example is found in the collection of Asbjørnsen and Moe (1886, 50).[9] In this version, there are two brothers, one rich and one poor; the rich brother tells the poor he can have a ham if he does what he asks, but then tells him to go to the devil with the ham he throws at him; he does so, and is rewarded with a wonder-mill that grinds anything. The elder brother buys the mill, but cannot stop it; he has to pay again for his poorer sibling to take it back. A sea captain then buys the wonder-mill from the erstwhile poor brother, and bids it grind salt, but does not know how to stop it, so it sinks and is still grinding. A similar tale is told in Iceland (Jón Árnason 1863–4, II 9–13), but here the rich brother buys the mill and sails away with it, but cannot stop it milling salt after giving it the command to do so.

The story of Grotti as reported by Snorri has clearly taken elements from this folktale: Mýsingr fills the role of the sea-captain who steals the mill and cannot stop it grinding salt. The poem itself, however, does not contain the theme of the salt-mill. The mill is represented as breaking at the end of the poem (and so could not continue functioning as a salt-mill), and its breaking mirrors the

[9] A parallel example from Hanover is given by Bolte and Polívka (1913, II 439), where the tale of the wonder-mill concludes with the mill's theft by a sea captain, who bids it grind salt, but cannot get it to stop, with the result that the ship sinks, drowning the crew and making the sea salt.

breaking of the *Fróða friðr* and the downfall of the tyrant. The poem could not coherently end anywhere other than where the extant text concludes. Whilst the demise of the mill in the ocean may be ancient, it is reasonable to suggest that the motif of the salt-mill became attached to Grotti only at a later time, when the deeper mythological significance of the mill had been forgotten; this was obviously before the time of Snorri, but perhaps not very long before. Alternatively, if Grotti was already associated with the salt-mill folktale, then the poet has deliberately avoided mentioning it.

Grotti of the poem differs in another aspect too. The mill of the folktale is a wonder-mill: it produces 'wealth' (in a wide sense), like Grotti, but, unlike Grotti, it works on its own. Grotti is thus only partially a wonder-mill; it is an ordinary mill to the extent that it requires two hefty giant girls to work it. The basic motif of the mill therefore differs between the poem and the folktale.

The cosmic mill

One of the best-developed notions of cosmic churning – of the turning of the central support of the cosmos (pillar or mountain) to produce the sustaining necessities of life (as well as misfortune) – is found in Indian myth.[10] Here, in a complex and extended series of episodes, the gods and demons contend with each other in churning the primeval milk ocean with an outlier of the world mountain, and by doing so produce many of the main cosmic entities such as the sun and moon – and also the elixir of well-being, *soma*, as well as unwelcome things like poison. Clearly there is an essential similarity with the tale of Grotti, milling out the gold which sustains the paradisal peace of Fróði, and then an army which destroys him. Yet there is nothing overtly cosmic about Grotti's make-up or achievements, and the tale is only lifted onto a mythological (or potentially religious) level through the implied association with a divine golden age. It would be unwise to overstate the case for seeing the tale of Grotti as a Germanic reflection of the Indian cosmic myth of the churning of the milk ocean.

Geographically and temporally closer than the Indian analogue to the tale of Grotti is the Finnish myth of the *sampo*,[11] a myth which may indeed ultimately owe something to an Indo-Iranian origin, for the word *sampo* may be borrowed from a proto-Iranian word *stambhas*, the (world) pillar.[12] In the case of the Finnish myth we are on firmer ground in seeing a cosmic dimension than in the Norse counterpart.

[10] The myth is recounted in the *Mahābhārata*; I have consulted O'Flaherty's translation (1975, 274–80). She gives the passages translated as being from the *Mahābhārata* I.15.5–13; I.16.1–40; I.17.1–30; 7 lines after I.61.35; 3 lines after I.61.32; 3 lines after I.16.36; 3 lines after I.16.40; 3 lines after I.17.7.

[11] I have dealt in detail with the Finnish myth of the *sampo* as an analogue of the Norse mill in Tolley 1994–5; what follows is largely a summary of this discussion.

[12] The proto-Iranians are thought to have lived much further to the west and north than modern Iran at the likely time of the loan, *c.* 2500 BC; *sampo* is one among several loans (including, for example, *taivas*, 'heaven') indicating a strong religious influence from the proto-Iranians (Koivulehto 1999, 230, 232).

The *sampo* is the subject of a core of traditional poems existing in a great many variants,[13] yet it is never described in detail in these poems, nor is its precise function determined. Its general effect was to ensure the wealth – but final destruction or detriment – of the possessor. Three poems, going back, it is believed, to at least AD 800, were fused into a sequence by 1200 (Kuusi 1949, 350–2; the dates are open to debate, but are based on factors such as distribution and variance of variants, on preservation of elements of archaic pagan belief, and on comparison with other folk poems relating to more firmly datable events): the Creation of the World, the Forging of the Sampo, and the Theft of the Sampo. In outline, the contents are:

The Creation of the World. Väinämöinen, the primordial sage, is shot by an enemy and drifts wounded for several years at sea where he performs various acts of creation. *The Forging of the Sampo.* Finally, he is washed ashore at Pohjola, whose mistress undertakes to return him to his own people on condition that he forges her a *sampo*. He promises that his fellow hero the smith Ilmarinen will do this and is allowed to return home. Ilmarinen agrees to forge the *sampo*, in return for which he is told he will receive the daughter of the mistress of Pohjola. Thus the *sampo* is made and provides the inhabitants of Pohjola with great wealth (in some versions explicitly by grinding). *The Theft of the Sampo.* Jealous of this, Väinämöinen and Ilmarinen set sail for Pohjola and steal the *sampo*. They are pursued and a furious battle takes place at sea, during which the mistress of Pohjola transforms herself into a *vaakalintu* (griffon), the *sampo* is smashed and the pieces are lost at sea. These and some fragments that are washed ashore bring fertility to land and sea.

The song was sung at the spring sowing (*Suomen kansan vanhat runot* I.1, 88b): Jyrkini Iivana related that 'when the spring sowing was done, first the sowing words were sung and then the song of the forging and theft of the sampo, and of the pursuit of the Mistress of Pohjola'. There is thus a clear implication that recounting the tale of this wealth-producing object would strengthen the crops to ensure the well-being of the community.

There have been innumerable interpretations of the word *sampo*, most of them implausible. The word is in derivation an adjectival formation from *sampa*, which originally appears to have signified 'pillar' (Setälä 1932, 479).[14] *Sammakko*, 'mill base', is another derivative from *sampa*; it means 'that which supports a *sampa*', i.e. the support for the mill's central axle. Drawing on the apparently parallel sense of *sammakko*, *sampo* is likely to have been interpreted as 'something fitted with a *sampa*', i.e. a mill; in origin, however, it probably meant '*sampa* object'. Harva (1943, 101–4) offers the most convincing interpretation of this: the *sampo* is a cult representation of the world-pillar; such representations are found widely in Siberia (Holmberg 1922–3, 9–33). The world-pillar is generally visualised as unmoving (Harva 1943, 42), and the *sampo* differs in this respect. However, the connection of the word *sampa* with mills must have

[13] Four versions of the Finnish *sampo* poems are given in Kuusi, Bosley and Branch 1977, nos. 12–15; see also the commentary there (526).

[14] Lönnrot (1958) records a saying in which *maasampa* means 'world pillar'; the derivative *sammas* in Vote and Estonian means 'pillar', but in Finnish 'stone'.

affected the concept of the world-pillar among the Finns; the Indian myth of the churning of the milk ocean demonstrates the plausibility of connecting the world-pillar with a productive milling motion. Although by the time of recorded poems the Finns had largely lost the concept of a world-pillar, a piecing together of the evidence reveals a consistent picture. Closely associated with the *sampo* is the *kirjokansi*, 'speckled lid'; *kansi* is used for 'sky' in the folk poetry. Since the North Star was referred to as the 'nail of the north' (preserved in the Estonian *pǫhjanael*), it seems the lid of the sky was fixed to the world pillar at the North Star, about which it turned. This turning came to be conceived as a sort of milling action, referred to as *sammasjauho* (*sampo*/pillar grinding). The *sampo* is naturally situated in Pohjola, because this is 'North Land', near the North Star. The tale of its removal by the heroes is an explanation of why the seasons now progress uneasily without the level of productiveness of the golden age: the *sampo*'s being moved from its position represents the uneven turning of the earth about its axis, observed in the progression of the seasons. The actual shattering of the *sampo* would seem to mark a complete destruction, which is inappropriate for the world-pillar (though it might apply to a cult image of the pillar), but this element of the tale is believed to have been influenced by the shattering of the egg in the myth of creation; originally the *sampo* was probably broken or set askew, but not shattered.

Grotti may show little indication of being a form of world pillar (as the *sampo* appears to be), or of carrying out its milling on a mythologically significant cosmic level, yet both motifs may be glimpsed elsewhere in Norse poems.

A cryptic hint of mythologically significant milling (but unconnected to any notion of the world pillar, as far as the evidence goes) is given in *Vafþrúðnismál*, though the text is highly obscure. The giant Vafþrúðnir says (st. 35):

Ørófi vetra	Numberless winters
áðr væri iǫrð um skǫpoð,	before the world was fashioned
þá var Bergelmir borinn;	Bergelmir was born;
þat ek fyrst of man,	the first thing I remember
er sá inn fróði iǫtunn	is when that wise giant
var á lúðr um lagiðr.	was laid on the mill-crib.

Bergelmir is the last of a threesome of primordial giants, Aurgelmir, Þrúðgelmir, Bergelmir. Stanza 35 appears to span Bergelmir's life: the laying in a mill-crib thus marks the end of the giant's life. There have been attempts at explaining away the sense 'mill-crib' for *lúðr*, so that a connection with milling cannot be regarded as certain.[15] However, taking *lúðr* in its literal sense of 'mill-crib' yields an extraordinary, but not unparalleled, motif of a giant being ground up. Any interpretation of the three giants is bound to remain tentative, particularly in view of the uncertainty of the meaning of the names. Fulk argues (1989, 317) that

[15] Christiansen suggests (1952, 101–5) that *lúðr* could mean 'cradle' here, on the basis of modern Norwegian *lur* (from Old Norse *lúðr*); it would seem inept, however, to describe a baby as *fróðr*. Holtsmark (1946, 53) proposed that *lúðr* could signify 'coffin'; since *ǫrk* can mean both 'coffin' and 'ark', Snorri could have invented the story he gives of how Bergelmir was saved with his household in the flood by climbing aboard his *lúðr* by association between *ǫrk* and *lúðr*.

aur- may be related to English *ear* (of corn). *Vafþrúðnismál* 33 tells that beneath Aurgelmir's arm grew a girl and boy together: limb begat on limb a six-headed son. This is presumably the son Þrúðgelmir, whose name is derived from *þrúðr*, 'might'. Fulk argues that the six-headed son is a six-headed ear of (emmer) wheat. Bergelmir is to be interpreted as containing *barr*, 'barley' (alternating forms *baraz-/bariz-* in Germanic explain the vowel difference); a more common interpretation sees the name as standing for Berggelmir, Mountain roarer. Moreover, Aurgelmir is more naturally interpreted as containing *aurr*, fertile mud coming from water (cf. *eyrr*, 'river-bank'): the poem recounts that he was formed from the coagulation of the primordial waters, Élivágar. The element *-gelmir*, 'roarer', characterises anything that roars loudly, in particular giants and torrential waters (as in Vaðgelmir and Hvergelmir, the source of all waters beneath the world-tree, and the related Gjǫll, the underworld river). *Aurgelmir* appears to connect these two sorts of roaring entity in one being. Thus a motif may underlie the account of *Vafþrúðnismál* in which the fertile earth, *aurr*, emerging from water (cf. the raising of earth from ocean in *Vǫluspá* 4; see commentary in *PE* II), produces grain, which thrives (*þrúðr*), and is then ground up as barley (Bergelmir on the *lúðr*). The implication is that the origins of fertility lay in the primordial or underworld waters. The main objection to Fulk's line of argument is that giants, while associated with sources of fertility, are not themselves producers of well-being (except when forced, as in *Grottasǫngr*).

The idea of being ground in a quern is implicit in *Lokasenna* 44, where it is said of Byggvir, a name also derived from the word for 'barley', *at eyrom Freys mundu æ vera ok und kvernom klaka*, 'you will for ever be at Freyr's ears and cluck under the quernstones'. There is no association with giants here, however. Clearer, but geographically remote, analogues can be found in the Middle East; in tenth-century Haran the pagans believed that fertility was secured by the god Tammuz being ground up by his master (al-Nadim 1970, 758), and in ancient Ugaritic sources Anat, on behalf of the fertility god Baal, grinds up their enemy Mot in what appears to be an act of splitting and parching grain for brewing (Wyatt 1998, 136). In England, the folksong 'The Passion of the Corn' may provide an analogue (and indeed possible descendant) of Byggvir in the person of John Barleycorn, ground up to provide food and drink.

Yet more difficult to interpret are some lines relating the tale of Mundilfœri in *Vafþrúðnismál* 23;[16] here we are presented with an image of the turning heavens, and possibly a 'handle', a variant of the world pillar. We do not have any actual grinding here.

Mundilfœri heitir,	He is called Mundilfœri,
hann er Mána faðir	the father of Moon
ok svá Sólar it sama;	and also of Sun;
himin hverfa	they are to turn heaven
þau skulo hverian dag	every day
ǫldom at ártali.	for the reckoning of years for men.

[16] The interpretation of *Vafþrúðnismál* 23 given here is based on that of Dronke, in her note to *Vǫluspá* 5/1–4 in *PE* II.

The meaning of the name *Mundilfœri* is open to interpretation, but Cleasby and Vigfusson (1957, *s.v. Mundilföri*) suggest that the name's first element is 'akin to *möndull* [mill-handle], referring to the veering round or revolution of the heavens', so the meaning would be 'mover of the handle' or 'effective with the handle' or 'handle device' (see Fritzner 1886–1972, *s.v. fœri*, for the senses); a connection with *mund*, 'time' is also possible, especially in view of the comment in the latter part of the stanza. It is thus possible (as I argued in Tolley 1994–5) that the myth of Mundilfœri envisaged the sky being turned by means of a handle-like device, in this case to express a concept of the determining of time, the beneficent seasons (*ár* signifying both senses), where the 'handle' could be a version of the world support. The regulation of time through a turning motion in order to produce welfare (*ár*) – directly paralleled in *Vǫluspá* 6–8, where the gods meet on Iðavǫllr, 'Eddy field' (see *PE* II, 118–19 for this interpretation of this admittedly obscure name), and apportion the times of day before enjoying their riches – is clearly analogous to the motif of the wealth and security milled out by Grotti, yet, in its extant form, the Grotti myth is not interested in the temporal regulation that, for the poets of *Vafþrúðnismál* and *Vǫluspá*, underlies abundance.

In Norse mythological tradition, then, we find (if the above interpretations of the meagre evidence are accepted) both the notion of the grinding of corn as a symbol of cosmic abundance, and (but distinct from the previous one) the image of the cosmos turning, or being turned with a handle (reminiscent of the Eurasian mythical world pillar), in such a way as to regulate time and the abundance of the seasons which depends upon this regulation. Grotti, however, is primarily an adaptation of the wonder-mill – the mill of folktales which grinds whatever its master bids. It assumes an aura of the cosmic, the mythic, only by allusion to motifs such as the gold-spangled reign of the King of Peace and the demiurgic giants which have taken on a cosmic significance (through association with the image of the gods' age of plenty). By contrast, the *sampo* must once have formed an integral part of traditional Finnish cosmology; it shows the signs of its high origin in the sustaining pillar of the cosmos, but in the extant poems has been reduced to little more than a wonder-mill. The tales of both Grotti and *sampo* have been 'tainted' by the aetiological salt-mill motif of folklore, which lends a certain similarity between the tales, but essentially the Norse and Finnish mill legends are quite distinct;[17] thus Grotti, by the time it is represented in Norse tradition, plays a part in certain distinct mythological situations not represented in Finnish myth, such as the mill's derivation from the chthonic world of the giants, represented as antagonists of the gods or orderly society of men, and the legendary fall of the house of Fróði. The Finnish and Indian analogues are of interest chiefly in demonstrating the differences in legendary or mythological realisations of the concept of the mill that are found in different societies.

[17] As I have argued previously (Tolley 1994–5), the acceptance by Finnish scholars (see for example Kuusi, Bosley and Branch 1977, 527–8) of Lid's proposal (1949) that the tale of the *sampo* derives (at least in many particulars) from Norse sources does not bear close scrutiny; once we are left with little more than a vague similarity between Grotti and *sampo* as common-place folktale wonder-mills, there is little reason to postulate much, if any, influence between the mythologems in any essential aspects (whilst admitting the possibility that some of the more peripheral details may perhaps have constituted motifs shared between these neighbouring lands).

Conclusion

We may now hazard some ideas about the connection between King Fróði and the mill Grotti.

The fertility gods Nerthus and Freyr both undertook perambulations among their people; Fróði was probably believed to do the same – certainly his dead body was carried around his realms after his death in what must have been a ritual act of blessing. This visitation is to be related to the cycle of the seasons, and in particular to the passage of the sun (the cart which carried Nerthus reminds us of the Trundholm waggon, with its gilded wheels and large disc, surely meant to represent the sun). The time of peace and prosperity under Fróði was no doubt a later reflection of the ritually enacted season of peace which obtained during Nerthus' visitation, as well as being comparable to the mythical time of plenty of the primordial gods in *Vǫluspá* 6–8, where the whirring cycle of time and cosmos is represented by the gods' meeting place, Iðavǫllr, and to the abundance of the seasons brought about by the activity of Mundilfœri, 'turner of the handle' of the world in *Vafþrúðnismál* 23.

We might well envisage that another image for the same turning around of the seasons would be that of the cosmic mill, whereby the firmament revolves around the North Star in the manner of a hand-quern, the seasons resulting from this milling. The Finns appear in ancient times to have conceived the structure of the cosmos in this fashion; it would well explain the connection between the mill Grotti and the fertility king Fróði if the Norse also had this image. Yet, at least in the extant records, Grotti scarcely seems to have been possessed of such a lofty mythological role; rather, it appears that a folktale of the wonder-working mill has become associated with Fróði simply because both were guarantors of wealth or fertility.

It is a remarkable characteristic of nearly all fertility beings in the Norse area that they are associated with water. The earliest record is of Nerthus, who emerges from a lake, and returns there: the waters surely mark a deathly realm from which fertility emerges, a motif found in many Middle Eastern myths. Njǫrðr dwells at Nóatún, 'ship meadow' (*Grímnismál* 16). Ullr (Ollerus) was noted for his magical skills at sea in Saxo (III, iv.12). Ing in the Old English *Rune Poem* passed 'over the waves'. In *Skírnismál* Freyr woos Gerðr out of the courts of her father Gymir, the gaping ocean. Two accounts of the deaths of the various Fróðis stand out; the motif of a violent death by a wild animal is found with many fertility deities, but here the motif is specifically one of death by a wild beast from the sea; in the one case this is explicit, in that a sea-cow slays Frotho III with its tusks, in the other it is implicit, in that Fróði is said to be killed by Mýsingr, described as a sea-captain by Snorri, but whose name is linked to 'mouse'.[18]

It is therefore noteworthy that in Finnish the *sampo* ends up in the sea, and the Norse Grotti likewise sinks, though this may have been a motif avoided by the author of the poem (Snæbjǫrn's verse, considered below, may, however,

[18] The connection of fertility gods with the sea is a huge topic; for a discussion of some key aspects, see Dronke 1998; I touch upon further ideas (primarily as they relate to Old English) in Tolley 1996.

imply that it was an ancient motif). The sea appears to be the destination of whatever engenders fertility, be it the demigod king, or the mechanical means of its production.

The motif of the destructive giantesses is specifically Norse; it is consistent with the presentation of giantesses in *Vǫluspá*, wishing to deprive gods and men of the fruits of well-being.

The motif of being ground up is found in association with some fertility gods; the myth of Bergelmir possibly reflects this in Norse (but this may equally well be a faulty interpretation). It does not seem that the fertility god himself is ground up in Norse, however. Nonetheless, the association of Byggvir with Freyr indicates at least that fertility gods and milling were associated,[19] making a deep-rooted connection between Fróði and Grotti all the more likely.

The kernel of the poem may be a very old concept: the turning of the corn-mill, and its falling and cracking off its proper pedestal, being an ancient metaphor within agricultural societies for an imagined erstwhile era of luxury and its subsequent loss, a metaphor which in certain traditions takes on a cosmic significance through its association with the turning of the heavens, and consequently the seasons, above the earth.

VI. *The poetic background, and date and place of composition*

The skaldic tradition

Relevant kennings for gold, in roughly chronological order (only the first three are from poems attributed to the pagan period), are:

Fróða mjǫl, 'Fróði's meal' (Egill Skallagrímsson, *Hǫfuðlausn* 17/8, *Skj* B I, 33);
Fróða þýja meldr, 'the grinding of Fróði's slave-girls' (Eyvindr Finnsson skáldaspillir, *lausavísa* 8, *Skj* B I, 64);
Fenju forverk, 'Fenja's menial work' (*Bjarkamál* 4/3, *Skj* B I, 170);
Fenju meldr, 'Fenja's grinding' (Þórmóðr Bersason Kolbrúnarskáld, *lausavísa* 24, *Skj* B I, 266; Einarr Skúlason, *Øxarflokkr* 6, *Skj* B I, 450; Snorri Sturluson, *Háttatal* 43, *Skj* B II, 73);
Fróða sáð, 'Fróði's seed' (Einarr Skúlason, *Øxarflokkr* 3, *Skj* B I, 450);

[19] Of interest (despite differences such as Fróði's not being explicitly young or prematurely killed) is the analogue noted by Krappe 1936, 54 (cf. Krappe 1924, 332): 'We furthermore know that a festival of general mourning was annually celebrated in Mysia, where it was connected with the name of King Kyzikos, said to have ruled over the Doliones in ancient times. Scholars are agreed in regarding him as one of those many youthful divinities doomed to a premature death: Hyakinthos, Hylas, Hippolytos, Attis, Adonis, etc., i.e. as a fertility daemon. He, too, is slain all of a sudden during a nightly invasion from the sea. Nor is this all. The most prominent feature of the annual festival commemorating Kyzikos seems to have been a grinding ritual, a ceremony where the celebrants, generally women, took a hand-mill and ground, accompanying their work with doleful dirges, the subject of which was King Kyzikos and his fatal death. It is not difficult to conjecture that such a ritual was known also in the North, as is proved by the mediaeval *cantilenae molares*, that one of the songs accompanying the rites was attached to the name of the god-king Frey-Fróði, and that it gave origin to the story of the grinding giantesses. In other words, the myth of Fróði's death is an aetiological tale explaining why the death of the mythical king was sung by grinding women at the grinding festival held in commemoration of this death and the end of the golden age.'

Fróða meldr, 'Fróði's grinding' (Rǫgnvaldr jarl Kolsson, *lausavísa* 15, *Skj* B I, 482);
Fróða fagrbygg, 'Fróði's fair barley' (*Óláfs drápa Tryggvasonar* 25, *Skj* B I, 573);
Fróða friðbygg, 'Fróði's peace barley' (Snorri Sturluson, *Háttatal* 43, *Skj* B II, 73);
Grotta glaðdript, 'Grotti's glad drift' (Snorri Sturluson, *Háttatal* 43, *Skj* B II, 73);
Fenju fagrmjǫl, 'Fenja's fair meal' (*Njáls saga*, st. 24, *Skj* B II, 217);
Menju góð, 'Menja's good things' (the Eddic *Sigurðarkviða in skamma* 52).

The legend of *Grottasǫngr* is thus reflected in kennings for 'gold' from the pagan period on; Fróði and Fenja are mentioned, but Menja only once. Grotti occurs only in one kenning, which postdates *Grottasǫngr*, apart from the verse of Snæbjǫrn considered below. Rarely is any narrative element found; however, Einarr Skúlason's *Øxarflokkr* 6 (first half of twelfth century) reads: *frák at Fróða meyjar fullgóliga mólu [. . .] grafvitnis beð*, 'I have heard that Fróði's maidens ground quite joyfully the serpent's bed [gold]' (*Skj* B I, 450). This is in direct opposition to other sources, which stress the misery of the girls – unless it reflects the tradition of st. 5–6 of *Grottasǫngr*, where the girls seem glad to be grinding out wealth. The fact that the same poem contains two more kennings for gold from the Grotti legend is explained by the fact that gold is the central theme of the work.

One of our earliest sources, Eyvindr skáldaspillir, cleverly contrasts two images derived from the myth of gold as corn (I follow Davidson 1983, 205–6):

Bárum Ullr um alla
ímunlauks á hauka
fjǫllum Fýrisvalla
fræ Hákonar ævi;
nú hefir folkstríðir Fróða
fáglýjaðra þýja
meldr í móður holdi
mellu dolgs um folgin.

God of the battle-leek [warrior], we used to carry the corn of Fýrisvellir [gold] on our hawks' hills [arms] during all the life of Hákon; now an enemy of the people (i.e. Haraldr Eiríksson) has hidden the flour of the joyless bondwomen of Fróði [gold] in the flesh of the mother of the enemy of the giantess [earth].

This indicates that Fróði was regarded as oppressive towards his slave-girls, and probably was seen as an enemy of the people like King Haraldr (note the juxtaposition of *folkstríðir Fróða*); the indications are that Fróði's golden age was regarded as collapsing in strife (see Davidson 1983, 206).

Snæbjǫrn's verse on Grotti

The only mention of Grotti earlier than *Grottasǫngr* is in a stanza (probably not originally a *lausavísa*) by one Snæbjǫrn, whose identity is unknown; a tenth- to eleventh-century date is likely:[20]

[20] *Skj* B I, 201. Gollancz (1898, xvii) suggested he was the arctic adventurer Snæbjǫrn Hólmsteinsson, mentioned in *Landnámabók* 190–5. I consider Snæbjǫrn's verse more fully in Tolley 1994–5, 69–71.

Hvatt kveða hrœra Grotta
hergrimmastan skerja
út fyr jarðar skauti
eylúðrs níu brúðir,
þær es, lungs, fyr lǫngu
líðmeldr, skipa hlíðar
baugskerðir rístr barði
ból, Amlóða mólu.

They say the nine brides [waves] of the island mill-crib [ocean] turn vigorously a most army-cruel Grotti of the skerries [whirlpool], out at the rim of the earth [ocean], they who long since have ground the meal [sand] of Amlóði's liquor [sea]. The ring-diminisher [prince] cuts with the prow of his vessel the habitation of the hillside of ships [waves].

The sea is pictured here as fiercely grinding up the land as a mill does meal. The sea is an *eylúðr*, island mill-crib, since it surrounds islands in the way the flat *lúðr* surrounds the quernstones upon it; a similar image (without the mill element) underlies *jarðar skaut*, 'rim, i.e. surrounder, of land'. Sand is pictured as the meal resulting from the milling action of the sea (the kenning is explained by reference to Saxo III, vi.10, where Amlethus, feigning madness, says that the sand is *farra* [. . .] *albicantibus maris procellis permolita*, 'meal ground fine by the hoary tempests of the sea'). 'Grotti of the skerries' may be another kenning for 'ocean', seen as the grinder-up of skerries. But the reference is surely more specific: this Grotti is *hergrimmastan*, 'the most army-cruel', because, it is to be assumed, it swallows armies on board perishing ships – or because it ground out an army to destroy Fróði, as *Grottasǫngr* reports. Snorri's explanation that a whirlpool arose from the eye of the sunken Grotti is surely relevant here: Snæbjǫrn means specifically an ocean whirlpool by 'Grotti of the skerries', the skerries in question being the hidden treacherous rocks below water which cause the currents, and which were imagined as being a sunken quern. The use of the superlative may suggest that Snæbjǫrn has a particular whirlpool in mind, but we cannot be certain. In any case it is situated 'out at the rim of the earth', a phrase which, if taken merely as a kenning for 'ocean' becomes rather otiose: it is probably meant to bear a literal sense as well. The prince is thus pictured not merely as crossing the ocean, but as crossing distant reaches of the ocean made perilous by a mighty whirlpool.

Snæbjǫrn's verse is important, for it shows that Snorri is unlikely to have invented the tale of Grotti's demise in the ocean; Snorri has tacked this story onto his summary of *Grottasǫngr*, which had no use for the tale, as it reaches its conclusion with the fall of Fróði. Analogues considered above indicate that the wonder-working mill is likely from the earliest times to have been thought of as perishing in the ocean. The poet of *Grottasǫngr* has drawn on only part of the ancient tale for his account. Snæbjǫrn's verse tends also to suggest that the motif of the mill grinding out an army against Fróði is an ancient element of the story.

Darraðarljóð

Grottasǫngr is represented as a worksong (though it is not comparable with actual worksongs recorded from many oral traditions): it is explicity said to accompany the work of milling. Such songs – which are primarily the preserve of women – must have been commonplace in Viking, as in other, societies,[21] yet we have only one other poem of a comparable nature in Old Norse. *Darraðarljóð* (again, really a pseudo-worksong) is cited in full in ch. 157 of *Njáls saga*. It is explained in the prose that a certain Dǫrruðr saw some women in a bower working at a loom, but instead of cloth, they were weaving men's entrails, and men's heads were the loom-weights. It is said that the vision coincided with the Battle of Clontarf in 1014. In his edition of the poem Poole shows that the verse does not warrant the interpretation given in the saga's prose (Poole 1991, 120–5). Dǫrruðr is probably an invention, formed from the word *darraðar* (genitive), an archaic word for 'pennant', that occurs in the poem. There is no indication of a bower, and it seems rather that the valkyries, the women doing the weaving, are in fact engaged in battle. The poem is relating the course of a battle, which is described using the metaphor of weaving at a loom. It uses the framework of a song accompanying weaving, but the work is in reality slaughter rather than weaving. Moreover, the poem may originally have commemorated an earlier battle, in 919, in which the Irish were decisively defeated. The structure of the poem is thus description of the battle, in terms of weaving (st. 1–3); the valkyries' avowal of support for the 'young king', accompanied by a worksong refrain *vindum, vindum vef darraðar*, 'let us wind, let us wind the weaving of the pennant' (st. 4–6); a series of prophecies resulting from the battle and the poem's conclusion (st. 7–11). These prophecies are that death lies in store for the great king, that the dwellers of the headlands will rule the lands, that the Irish will grieve, and that news of the disaster will travel across the land. The actual end of the battle is marked in st. 8 with the statement *nú er vefr ofinn en vǫllr roðinn*, 'now the fabric is woven and the field dyed red'. The poem concludes with the valkyries exclaiming 'let us ride hence with brandished swords', that is away from the battle described and on to others.

The author of *Njáls saga* has interpreted the whole poem as a supernatural representation of the battle, however, in which an actual task of weaving with men's bodies determines the outcome of the fight; in some sense the valkyries are seen as both present in the battle and determining it from outside.[22]

The outline structure of *Grottasǫngr* is: arrival and setting up of the quern

[21] That songs accompanied milling is specifically mentioned in *Haraldssona saga* ch. 18 (ÍF 28, 325), where King Sigurðr, riding in Vík, hears singing so beautiful that he seeks out the house it is coming from, and there *stóð kona ein við kvern ok kvað forkunnar fagrt, er hon mól*, 'a woman stood by the quern and sang remarkably well as she milled'. Sigurðr sleeps with the woman, named Þóra, who then bears a son named Hákon. The richness of women's worksongs is exemplified in the Gaelic waulking songs of the Scottish islands (themselves once Norse) preserved into the present century: see the large collection of waulking songs in Campbell and Collinson 1969–81.

[22] Compare the game of *gwyddbwyll* between Arthur and Owain in *The Dream of Rhonabwy* in the *Mabinogion* (slightly earlier than *Njáls saga*, which is probably late thirteenth century: *Njáls saga* lxxxiv), where it is implied that the moves in the game correspond to the developments in the battle.

(st. 1–4); the gladsome declaration, beginning with the worksong-like exhortation *mǫlum* [. . .] *mǫlum* (st. 5), of the riches to be milled for the king (st. 5–6); interjection of the king (st. 7); recounting of the giantesses' life – the uncovering of the quernstones, the engagement in battle as *framvísar tvær*, 'two foresighted women', the arrival in misery at Fróði's (st. 8–17); the continuing milling, with the worksong-like refrain *mǫlum enn framarr* in 21–2, as a hostile army attacks Fróði, and the prophecy that he will lose his throne (st. 17–22); the collapse of the mill (st. 23); the final statement by the girls that the milling is completed (st. 24).

Some of the structural elements of *Darraðarljóð* may have influenced *Grottasǫngr*. The stanzas of support for Fróði (st. 5–6) match those of support for the young king by the valkyries; and as *Darraðarljóð* switches to prophesying death for the mighty king (his opponent), *Grottasǫngr* predicts the downfall of the king, Fróði (st. 20). The declaration that the fabric is woven, intimating that the battle is over (*Darraðarljóð* 8), corresponds to the concluding statement of the giant girls that *malit hǫfum* [. . .] *sem munum hætta*, 'we have milled so that we shall stop', from which we understand that the vengeance is assured. One of the weakest structural elements of *Grottasǫngr* is the engagement in wars in Sweden by the 'two foresighted women' (st. 13–15); this confirms the girls' warrior status, but not their foresight (which may even be referred to ironically), and the emphasis on the episode seems excessive. On the other hand, the engagement in battle by the foresighted valkyries forms the central theme of *Darraðarljóð*. It would seem likely that the poet of *Grottasǫngr* wished to appropriate some of the awe of these prophetic valkyries by incorporating an episode of slaughterous activity conducted by the 'foresighted' giantesses. Two phrases in the poem suggest borrowing from *Darraðarljóð*. The giantesses say (st. 13/4) *í fólk stigum*, 'we strode into battle', just as the valkyries say *fram skulum ganga ok í fólk vaða*, 'we must go forth and advance into battle' (*Darraðarljóð* 4/5–6); and, describing the loom, it is said that *járnvarðr yllir*, 'the shed rod is ironclad' (meaning it is a weapon) (*Darraðarljóð* 2/7), just as when the quern breaks to pieces it is despite the *støðr*, 'supports', being *iárni varðar*, 'ironclad' (st. 21/7).

Grottasǫngr differs from *Darraðarljóð* in various respects. The valkyries express support for a young king and predict the downfall of his opponent, whereas the mill in *Grottasǫngr* churns out both blessings and misfortunes for the same king, and Mýsingr is no more than an implied agent of the giantesses' vengeance against Fróði. In addition, there is no question but that the giantesses are actually milling: therefore it is their action of milling which produces the avenging army to overthrow Fróði. They also seem to envisage themselves as engaged in the fighting – *eruma valnar í valdreyra*, 'we are not squeamish in the blood of slaughter'. Thus the scene seems somewhat closer to the interpretation of the author of *Njáls saga*, a sort of simultaneous involvement in the milling which is determining the battle's fate, and in the fatal battle as it is being determined. A greater poet might, along the lines of *Darraðarljóð*, have imagined the act of mining gold and mastering the chthonic forces of the rocks in which it was found through the metaphor of the giantesses' milling, but the aspirations of the author of *Grottasǫngr* were clearly less lofty.

The heroic-verse context

An investigation of the vocabulary of *Grottasǫngr* reveals a series of analogues in Eddic heroic verse, but very few in mythological verse. Clearly the author regarded his work as belonging among the tales of men, not gods.

Elsewhere in Eddic poetry Fróði is mentioned only in *Helgakviða Hundingsbana I* 13, *sleit Fróða frið fiánda á milli; fara viðris grey valgirn um ey*, 'Fróði's peace was cut between enemies; Óðinn's wolves go about the isle eager for slaughter'. Other vocabulary is also reflected in the *Helgakviður* (see commentary to 16/7, 19/3, 20/4). It is likely that *vígspiǫll* (19/3) is borrowed from *Helgakviða Hundingsbana II*, where it is used more aptly. The most striking parallel is with st. 2–4 of *Helgakviða Hundingsbana II*, which (with the preceding prose) read:

> Hamall hét sonr Hagals. Hundingr konungr sendi menn til Hagals at leita Helga. En Helgi mátti eigi forðaz annan veg en tók klæði ambǫttar ok gekk at mala. Þeir leitoðo ok fundo eigi Helga. Þá kvað Blindr inn bǫlvísi:
>
> Hamall was the name of Hagall's son. King Hundingr sent some men to Hagall to search for Helgi. Helgi could not escape danger any other way than by putting on the attire of a servant girl and going to grind. They searched and did not find Helgi. Then Blindr the mischief-causer said:

'Hvǫss ero augo í Hagals þýio, era þat karls ætt er á kvernom stendr: steinar rifna, støkkr lúðr fyrir!	'Sharp are the eyes on Hagall's slave-girl, that is no working-man's lineage standing at the quern: the stones are cracking, and the corn-crib flies loose before her!
Nú hefir hǫrð dœmi hildingr þegit, er vísi skal valbygg [mala]; heldr er sœmri hendi þeiri meðalkafli en mǫndultré.'	Now the prince has received a harsh sentence: the ruler must mill foreign barley; a swordhilt suits that hand rather better than a mill-handle.'

Hagall svaraði ok kvað: — Hagall answered and said:

'Þat er lítil vá, þótt lúðr þrumi, er mær konungs mǫndul hrœrir; hón skævaði skýiom efri ok vega þorði sem víkingar,	'It means little, even though the corn-bin thunders, as the king's daughter turns the handle; she used to dart over the clouds and dared to battle like the Vikings,

áðr hana Helgi	before Helgi
hǫpto gørði;	took her captive;
systir er hón þeira	she is the sister
Sigars ok Hǫgna,	of Sigarr and Hǫgni,
því hefir ǫtul augo	that's why the servant
Ylfinga man.'	of the Ylfings has sharp eyes.'

The scene may have influenced the poet of *Grottasǫngr.* Like Fenja and Menja in the poem (but without parallel elsewhere, and incidental even to the theme of the poem), according to Hagall the worker of the mill in *Helgakviða Hundingsbana II* is a noble woman used to engaging in battle before being captured by Helgi: and hence the quernstones are cracking and the whole apparatus shaking. This confirms the social aspect of *Grottasǫngr*: the foreign female war-captives put to menial work on the mill, and the resentment they undoubtedly felt. The shattering of Grotti – an event inconsistent with its subsequent role as a salt-mill in the ocean depths, which seems already to be a part of the folktale of Grotti by the time of Snæbjǫrn, but which the poet of *Grottasǫngr* has ignored – is perhaps an exaggeration of the harsh treatment Helgi gives the quern (though this may well not be the only source of this variant of the story of the mill). The word *valbygg* in *Helgakviða Hundingsbana II* 3/4 could also imply a meaning 'slaughter barley', which is effectively what the giantesses grind in *Grottasǫngr*.

The name *Gotþormr/Guttormr* is found in the heroic poems; as the name occurs along with *Knúi* only in a verse of *Ǫrvar-Odds saga* this must be considered a possible source (cf. also commentary to 13/8).

Other analogues are found with *Atlamál* (see commentary to 14, 16/8, 19/6; in st. 14 there is some possibility of influence from *Atlamál*), *Atlakviða* (see commentary to 16/7), *Grípisspá* (see commentary to 1/3, 15/5–6), *Sigrdrífumál* (see commentary to 6/7, 16/7), *Guðrúnarkviða I* (see commentary to 8/3), *Sigurðarkviða in skamma* (see commentary to 16/8). Some analogues in what might be termed 'semi-heroic' poems are also found: *Rígsþula* (see commentary to 16/5–6, 23/2), *Hárbarðsljóð* (see commentary to 16/8), *Hyndluljóð* (see commentary to 19/1); of these only *Rígsþula* 16/5–6 is significant, suggesting possible borrowing.

One likely borrowing from *Grottasǫngr* is found in Ívarr Ingimundarson (see commentary to 19/7–8), composing *c.* 1140, which would give a *terminus ante quem* for the poem's composition.

Other literary influences and parallels

It is likely that the poet was familiar with skaldic verse (see commentary to 9, 9/7, 11/8, 14/8, 15/5), but specific influence is only reasonably demonstrable in the cases of Egill (see commentary to 7/3–4, 16/7, also st. 6) and *Bjarkamál* (which recounted the fall of a successor of Fróði's, Hrólfr kraki) (see commentary to 18/4–5, 19). The expression *dólgs siǫtul*, though not in fact a kenning, may reveal a familiarity with skaldic technique (though compare similar phrases in Eddic verse: see commentary to 16/7).

It is difficult to trace influence from *Skjǫldunga saga* in the absence of the

Old Norse text, but it seems likely that the poet is alluding to descriptions of the golden age of Fróði that had already crystallised into a form resembling what is found in *Skjǫldunga saga* (see commentary to st. 6, also 11).

The date and place of composition

Several factors indicate a late date for the composition of *Grottasǫngr* in its extant form (even though, as has been shown, individual elements in the poem are likely to be of great antiquity). There is nothing of a mythological nature in the poem which challenges our understanding: indeed, there is little reflection of what must once have been a rich mythological field. Fróði is son of Friðleifr, which must be the result of genealogical speculation made after the end of paganism, and is in agreement with sources from the thirteenth century on. It seems that frið-Fróði and Heathobard Fróði are confused (perhaps deliberately) by the poet, as would scarcely have happened in the pagan period. There is an appeal to a tradition of the *Fróða friðr* similar to that of *Skjǫldunga saga*, most likely a twelfth-century work.[23] The poet shows a familiarity with heroic Eddic verse, some of it late (like *Atlamál*: probably twelfth century, see *PE* I, 111).

The vocabulary of the poem also indicates a late date. Some of it occurs chiefly in prose (see commentary to 9/7, 15/5, 19/6, 23/4); and there are three words which derive from the developed lexicon of Christianity (*alsæll* (5/2), *meginverkum* (11/6), *miskunnlausar* (16/3)), which point to a date not earlier than the twelfth century. If *Grottasǫngr* is indeed quoted around 1140, a date shortly before that would be most likely for its composition.

Guðrún Nordal (2001, 310), following Bjarni Guðnason, emphasises the importance of Danish royal history in the later twelfth century in Iceland (and implies that the Danish influence in fact stretches back to much earlier in the century):

> Throughout this study I have noted the eminence of Danish myths and legends in relation to skaldic poetry and during the earliest phase of the writing of royal *historia*. It is, I believe, no coincidence that this Danish bias is most recognizable in learned works on skaldic poetics – *Snorra Edda*, *Háttalykill*, and *Skáldatal* – as well as in the subject matter of poems preserved in, and in conjunction with, *Snorra Edda* in manuscripts (e.g., *Ragnarsdrápa*, *Jómsvíkingadrápa*, *Málsháttakvæði*, and *Rígsþula*). These texts suggest that the textual culture, and the study of skaldic poetics in particular, was subject to a decisive and unequivocal Danish influence. Why was this the case? Earlier we tentatively endorsed Bjarni Guðnason's view that this fascination with Danish history resulted from the formative influence of Lund on the education of Icelanders in the twelfth century. Lund was the archiepiscopal seat for Iceland until the establishment of the archbishopric at Niðaróss in 1153. Six Icelandic bishops, three at Hólar and three at Skálaholt, were consecrated at Lund in the twelfth century. [. . .] These cultural links with Lund and Denmark were not broken off after the founding of Niðaróss, but were actively maintained thereafter.

[23] Bjarni Guðnason suggests 1180–1200 in *Danakonunga sǫgur* lii.

Nordal notes (312) the convention in European historiography of this period to set the royal genealogy within a mythic framework, a convention followed for example by William of Malmesbury (d. *c.* 1142) and Geoffrey of Monmouth (d. *c.* 1154) and taken up in the preface to Snorri's *Edda*. Genealogy was a primary concern of the earliest vernacular writings in Iceland (beginning in the later eleventh century), according to the *First Grammatical Treatise* (fol. 84/14, p. 12).

It is surely within this period of focus upon Danish royal genealogy and its mythic background that *Grottasǫngr* as we have it was composed. The poem labours the point about the importance of genealogy; whilst the focus is upon the family history of the giantesses, this surely acts as a foil to the Danish king Fróði, whose ancestry, as has been noted, was a major source of fascination in historical works from the late twelfth century. The poem also appears, like *Rígsþula*, to be concerned with social order, in that Fróði suffers as a result of maltreatment of his slaves, whose real nature is belied by their menial status – *noblesse oblige*, and when that obligation is ignored it leads to disaster. It is not clear, however, that social concern of this sort can be used as a criterion of dating.

Given the likely date of the poem's composition in the twelfth century, I have treated it as essentially a literary product (though the shift from orality to literacy was certainly not a black-and-white affair); hence the many parallels found in other poems are treated as allusions or borrowings, rather than reflections of oral formulas, though it is, naturally, impossible to be certain that this was always the case.

There is no evidence to suggest firmly where the poem was composed. The existence of two words in the poem, *gria* and *vamlar* (or *valnar*), which are not Icelandic, and the fact that cuckoos are not found in Iceland,[24] suggests that the poem is not Icelandic. The word *valnar* (if we favour that reading) has a sense most appropriate to the poem in Norn. The word *grotti* also survived in Norn. Stories of Grotti Minnie and Grotti Finnie and their salt-quern in the Swelchie of the Pentland Firth survived on Orkney at least until 1895 (Johnston 1908–9, 297); Fenja and Menja had by then become witches, characters of local superstition used to frighten children.[25] Manuscripts A and B (AM 748, 757) of Snorri's *Edda*, in an addition to Snorri's work, recount the following (*SnE* 259):

> Kvern heitir Grótti, er átti Fróði konungr; hon mól hvetvetna þat er hann vildi, gull ok frið. Fenja ok Menja hétu ambáttir þær, er mólu. Þá tók Mýsingr sækonungr Gróttu ok lét mala hvítasalt á skip sín, þar til er þau sukku á Pétlandsfirði. Þar er svelgr síðan, er sær fellr í auga Gróttu. Þá gnýr sær, er hon gnýr, ok þá varð sjórinn saltr.
>
> A quern is called Grotti, which King Fróði possessed; it milled whatever he wished, gold and peace. Fenja and Menja were the names of the servant girls who milled. Then Mýsingr a sea-king took Grotta and had salt ground on his

[24] Cuckoos are mentioned by Egill and Snorri, however, both (travelled) Icelanders.

[25] This last echo of the tale of *Grottasǫngr* appears to have died away as soon as it was recorded; Tom Muir, an Orkney folklore researcher, is clear that no further tales of Fenja and Menja have been recorded from Orkney, so effective was the opposition from the local Kirk to Norn language and traditions (personal communication).

> ships, until they sank in the Pentland Firth. There has been a whirlpool there ever since, where the sea falls into the eye of Grotta. Then the sea grates as the mill grates, and then the sea became salty.

Clearly the connection between Grotti and the Orkney whirlpool called the Swelchie is old. It is at least possible that the poem was formed with these traditions behind it, though the whirlpool motif is explicitly excluded by the poet from his work.

Grottasǫngr

Sonr Friðleifs hét Fróði. Hann tók konungdóm eptir fǫður sinn í þann tíð er Augustus keisari lagði frið of heim allan; þá var Kristr borinn. En fyrir því at Fróði var allra konunga ríkastr á Norðrlǫndum þá var honum kendr friðrinn um alla danska tungu, ok kalla Norðmenn þat Fróða frið. Engi maðr grandaði ǫðrum, þótt hann hitti fyrir sér fǫðurbana eða bróðurbana lausan eða bundinn. Þá var ok engi þiófr eða ránsmaðr, svá at gullhringr einn lá á Ialangrsheiði lengi. Fróði konungr sótti heimboð í Svíðióð til þess konungs, er Fiǫlnir er nefndr. Þá keypti hann ambáttir tvær, er hétu Fenia ok Menia; þær vóru miklar ok sterkar. Í þann tíma fannz í Danmǫrk kvernsteinar tveir svá miklir, at engi var svá sterkr, at dregit gæti; en sú náttúra fylgði kvernunum, at þat mólz á kverninni, sem sá mælti fyrir, er mól. Sú kvern hét Grotti. Hengikiǫptr er sá nefndr, er Fróða konungi gaf kvernina. Fróði konungr lét leiða ambáttirnar til kvernarinnar ok bað þær mala gull, ok svá gerðu þær, mólu fyrst gull, ok frið ok sælu Fróða; þá gaf hann þeim eigi lengri hvíld eða svefn en gaukrinn þagði eða hlióð mátti kveða; þat er sagt, at þær kvæði lióð þau, er kallat er Grottasǫngr. Ok áðr létti kvæðinu, mólu þær her at Fróða, svá at á þeiri nótt kom þar sá sækonungr, er Mýsingr hét, ok drap Fróða, tók þar herfang mikit. Þá lagðiz Fróða friðr. Mýsingr hafði með sér Grotta ok svá Feniu ok Meniu ok bað þær mala salt; ok at miðri nótt spurðu þær, ef eigi leiddiz Mýsingi salt. Hann bað þær mala lengr. Þær mólu litla hríð, áðr niðr søkk skipit, ok var þar eptir svelgr í hafinu, er særinn fellr í kvernar augat; þá varð sær saltr.

The son of Friðleifr was named Fróði. He succeeded to the kingdom after his father at the time that the emperor Augustus imposed peace on the whole world; Christ was born then. As Fróði was most powerful of all kings in

The text of the poem is preserved only in manuscripts SR *and* T *(st. 1 also in* C*) of Snorri's Edda; the* SR *text is followed here, with variants from* C *and* T *noted. Each stanza begins with a capital in the manuscripts (unless noted otherwise in the textual notes), and in* SR *most helmingar are marked with* ⁝ T *also marks many helmingar in 8-line stanzas with a capital (not 1b, 2b, 6b, 8b, 9b, 11b (but preceded by point), 13b, 17b, 18b, 21b). In* T, *forms of* ð, d *are indistinguishable, and are transcribed here according to the sound in the context. A common source of misreadings in both manuscripts has been minim confusion; see st. 3/1, 3/4, 4/2, 8/4, 17/5, 19/6, 21/7. The prose introduction is standardised from SnE, where textual variants may be found listed.*

Conventions: IC *initial capital,* MC *marginal capital, italics: emendation,* [ ] *not in manuscript,* ⌊ ⌋ *reading from another manuscript,* ° *manuscript letter omitted in emendation,* † † *text transferred,* ` ´ *superscript addition in manuscript,* | *end of line in manuscript,* ÷ *omission,* + *addition. Underdots (representing deletions) are scribal.*

northern lands the peace was ascribed to him in all the Norse-speaking lands, and the Norsemen call it the peace of Fróði. No one harmed another, even if he chanced upon his father's or brother's slayer before him, free or bound. There was no thief or robber then, so a gold ring long lay upon Jalangrsheiðr. King Fróði visited a king called Fiǫlnir in Sweden. He bought two slave-girls named Fenia and Menia; they were big and strong. At that time two quernstones were found in Denmark, so big that no one could move them. It was a feature of the quernstones that they would grind out whatever the grinder told them to. This quern was called Grotti. Hengikiǫptr was the name of the one who gave Fróði the quernstones. King Fróði had the slave-girls led to the quern and ordered them to grind out gold, and so they did: they ground out gold first, and peace and well-being for Fróði. He gave them no more rest or sleep than a cuckoo is silent or it takes to sing a song. It is said that they sang the lay called 'The Song of Grotti'. And before the quern stopped they ground out an army against Fróði, so that at night there came a sea-king called Mýsingr, who slew Fróði and took great booty there. That was the end of Fróði's Peace. Mýsingr took Grotti with him and Fenia and Menia too, and he ordered them to grind salt. At midnight they asked if Mýsingr was not tired of salt. He ordered them to carry on milling. They milled for a little while until the ship sank. There was afterwards a whirlpool in the ocean where the sea fell into the eye of the quernstone: then the sea became salt.

1	'Nú erum komnar	'Now we have come
	til konungs húsa	to the king's houses,
	framvísar tvær,	far-sighted, both of us,
	Fenia ok Menia.'	Fenia and Menia.'
	Þær ro at Fróða,	They are at Fróði's,
	Friðleifs sonar,	Friðleifr's son,
	máttkar meyiar,	mighty maidens
	at mani hafðar.	kept as menials.
2	Þær at lúðri	To the mill-crib
	leiddar vóru	they were conducted,
	ok griótz griá	and the grit grindstones
	gangs of beiddu;	they goaded into motion.
	hét hann hvárigri	He promised to neither girl
	hvíld né ynði,	pause nor pleasure,
	áðr hann heyrði	before he heard
	hlióm ambátta.	the slave-women's harmony.

1/1 Nú] *large* IC SR, T 1/1 erum] *so* SR, T, eru C 1/5 ro] eru C 1/6 Friðleifs] frilleifs T 1/8 hafðar] gioruar C 2/3 griótz] grioz T 2/3 griá] gr`i´a T

3 Þær þyt þu*t*u
þǫgnhorf°nar:
'Leggium lúðra,
léttum steinum!'
Bað hann enn meyiar
at þær mala skyldu.

They started the screeching,
shunned by silence;
'Let us fix firm the mill-crib,
let us ease the stones!'
Again he urged the girls
to go on with the milling.

4 Sungu ok slungu
snúðga steini,
svá at Fróða man
flest sofnaði.
Þá kvað þat Meni[a],
– var til meldr[ar] komi*t*:

They sang and slung
the swift-swirling stone,
so that Fróði's servants
were mostly asleep.
Then Menia spoke
– the meal had started to flow:

5 'Auð mǫlum Fróða,
mǫlum alsælan,
⌊mǫlum⌋ fiǫlð fiár
á feginslúðri!
Siti hann á auði,
sofi hann á dúni,
vaki hann at vilia –
þá er vel malit!

'Let us grind riches for Fróði,
let us grind him all-fortunate,
let us grind massive wealth,
on the mill of felicity!
May he sit on riches,
may he sleep on down,
may he wake to joy –
then that is milling well done!

6 'Hér skyli engi
ǫðrum granda,
til bǫls búa
né til bana orka,
né hǫggva[g]i
hvǫssu sverði,
þó at bana bróður
bundinn finni!'

'Here must no one
harm another,
work for his ill-fortune
or encompass his death,
nor strike him any blow
with biting sword,
even though his brother's murderer
he should find in fetters!'

3/1–2 ÷T 3/1 þutu] þulu SR 3/2 þǫgnhorfnar] þæ͞o͞g|horviɴar SR 3/3 leggium] ɪc T 3/4 steinum] steuiū *(? i.e.* stefium, *cf.* heui *17/3, 24/3 (JH))* T 3/6 skyldu] scyldi T 4/2 snúðga] *so* T, stiuðga (*apparently; though* st *is abnormally formed, and may be a correction to* n *after an initial reading of* n *as* ti) SR 4/2 steini] steina T 4/5 Þá] ɪc T 4/5–6 Menia . . . meldrar] menia . . . meldrs T, meni . . . meldr SR 4/6 komit] kom̅ SR, comı̄ T 5/1 *no* ɪc SR, T 5/1 Auð] aul (*i.e.* ǫl) T 5/3 mǫlum] *so* T, ÷ SR 5/5 Siti] ɪc SR, T 6/5 -gi] *so* T, þ[vi] SR

7 En hann †⌊ekki⌋† kvað	No words he said
orð it fyrra:	sooner than these:
'Sofið eigi þit *me*[ir]	'Sleep no more, you two,
en s[yngr]a*t* gauk°r!	than the cuckoo stops singing,
eða lengr en svá	or longer than I chant
lióð eitt kveðak.'	a single charm.'
8 'Var⌊t⌋attu, Fróði,	'You were not, Fróði,
fullspakr of þik,	very far-sighted for yourself,
málvinr manna,	– mankind's sweetheart –
er þú man keyptir.	when you bought slaves.
Kaus⌊*t*⌋u at afli	You picked them for strength
ok at álitum,	and appearances,
en at ætterni	but as to their ancestry
ekki spurðir.	you asked no question.
9 'Harðr var Hrungnir	'Unyielding was Hrungnir
ok hans faðir –	and his father too –
þó var Þiazi	yet Þiazi proved
þeim ǫflgari.	more powerful than they.
Iði ok Aurnir,	Iði and Aurnir
okrir niðiar,	are our kinsmen,
brœðr bergrisa,	brothers of crag-giants:
þeim erum bornar.	we were born from their line.
10 'Kœmia Grotti	'Grotti would not have come
ór Griáfialli,	from the Grindstone Fell,
né sá hinn harði	nor that hard
hal⌊l⌋r ór iǫrðu,	rock from out of the earth,

7/1 ekki kvað] *so* T, qvað ecki SR 7/3–4 sofið — gaukr] *see Commentary on the emendations in these lines.* 7/3 þit] it T 7/3 meir] ne SR, T 7/4 en] of SR, T 7/4 syngrat] sal SR, T 7/4 gaukr] gavk^{ar} SR, gaucar T 7/6 eitt] eit SR, T 8/1 Vartattu] *so* T, Varattv SR 8/2 of] ū T 8/4 er] ef T 8/4 man] malj T *must derive from an antecedent scribal* maɴ (*cf. forms of* ɴ *in* SR), *influenced perhaps by* maɴa *in the previous line.* 8/5 kaustu] *so* T, kꜵssþv SR 8/8 ekki spurðir] eī sprðir T 9/5 Aurnir] ꜵrn^{ir} SR, aurnir T (*MS forms can also be read* Ǫrnir.) 9/7 brœðr] broðr T 10/1 Kœmia] Komi á T 10/2 griá fialli] griafalli T 10/3 hinn] in̄ T 10/4 hallr] *so* T, halr SR

né mœli svá
mær bergrisa,
ef vissi[m] vi*t*
vætr til *k*[v]e*r*nar.

nor would a crag-giant's girl
be doing such grinding,
if we two had known
nothing of the millstone.

11 'V*it* vetr níu
vórum leikur
ǫflgar, alnar
firir iǫrð neðan.
Stóðu[m] meyiar
at meginverkum,
[h*ó*fum] siálfar
setberg ór stað.

'For nine winters we two
were playfellows,
mighty girls, bred
beneath the earth.
As maidens we took on
tasks of great moment:
we ourselves plucked
the mountain-seat from its place.

12 'Veltum grióti
of garð risa,
svá at fold firir
fór skiálfandi.
Svá sløngðum vit
snúðga steini,
hǫfga halli,
at halir tóku.

'We sent the stone rolling
over the realm of giants,
so the ground before it
began to quake.
The two of us flung so far
the fast-wheeling stone,
the heavy rock,
that humans took it.

13 'En vit síðan
á Svíþióðu,
framvísar tvær,
í fólk stigum.
Bei[*tt*]um biǫrnu,
en brutum skiǫldu,
gengum í gegnum
gráserkiat li[*ð*].

'And since then we two
in Sweden,
far-sighted, both of us,
strode into battle.
We baited bears,
and hacked shields,
marched right through
their mail-clad host.

10/5 mœli] moli SR, meli T   10/7 vit] vit SR, vit T   10/8 kvernar] ħnar SR, ħn^{ar} T   11/1 Vit] Vær SR, Ver T   11/2 leikur] leikō T   11/5 stóðum] stoðv SR, stoðo T (m *omitted due to haplography before following* m *of* meyiar)   11/6 at] a T   11/7 hófum] færþv̄ SR, Haufō (*?for* hófom (*JH*), *with* ɪc) T   11/7 siálfar] sialfr sialf^{ar} T   12/5 sløngðum] slaungðu T   12/6 snúðga] snuðug T   13/2 Svíþióðu] sviðioðv SR, suiðioðo T   13/3 tvær] .ij. SR   13/4 fólk stigum] floc stigō folc stigō T   13/5 beittum] *so* T, beiddv̄ SR   13/8 lið] *so* T, lit SR

14 'Steyptum stilli,
studdum annan.
Veittum góðum
Got*þ*ormi lið.
Vara kyrrseta,
áðr Knúi felli.

'We toppled one prince,
propped up another.
To good Gotþormr
we gave our support.
There was no time of truce
till Knúi fell.

15 'Fram heldum því
þau misseri,
at vit at kǫppum
kendar vóru[m].
Þar skorðu[m] vit
skǫrpum geirum
blóð ór benium
ok brand ruðum.

'We pursued that life
throughout those seasons,
so that as champions
we both were acknowledged.
There we two carved
with keen spears
blood from wounds,
and made our blades red.

16 'Nú erum komnar
til konungs húsa
miskunnlausar
ok at mani hafðar.
Aurr etr iliar,
en ofan kulði.
Drǫgum dólgs siǫtul –
daprt er at Fróða!

'Now we have come
to the king's houses,
and without pity
have been put as slaves.
Mud corrodes our soles,
and cold nips from above.
Round we heave war's settler –
wretched it is at Fróði's!

17 'Hendr skulo hvílaz,
hallr standa mun.
Malit hefi ek firir mik
mitt of [h]le*y*ti!'
'[*M*]u[*n*]u[*m*]a hǫndum
hvíld vel gefa,
áðr fullmalit
Fróða þykki!

'Hands shall take rest,
stone will stand still.
For my part I have milled
in accord with my pledge!'
'We will not give
our hands good rest,
before the milling seems to Fróði
fully done!

14/1 *no* IC (*but point precedes*) SR, T 14/3 góðum] vit^{ro}m T 14/4 Gotþormi] gotHormi SR, guðormi T 15/4 vórum] *so* T, v̊ SR 15/5 skorðum] skorþv SR, scerðo T 16/1 erum] e^{ro} T 16/3 miskunnlausar] miscunlausar T 16/4 at] ÷T 16/5 aurr] Aur T 16/7 dólgs] dogls T (*cf. Vǫluspá 41/6* gagl/galg) 16/8 daprt] darptr T 17/1, 18/1 Hendr] Hendor T 17/2 mun] mon T 17/3 hefi] heui T 17/4 hleyti] leiti SR, T 17/5 munuma] *so* T, nv mvna SR 17/5 hǫndum] + heldr T

18 ‘Hendr skulo hǫ*n*†*d*†la
harðar triónor,
vápn valdreyrug –
vaki þú, Fróði!
Vaki þú, Fróði,
ef þú †⌊vill⌋† hlýða
sǫngum okkrum
ok sǫgum fornum!

‘Hands shall handle
hard staves,
slaughter-gory weapons –
wake up, Fróði!
Wake up, Fróði,
if you want to hear
the songs we two sing
and stories of old!

19 ‘Eld sé ek brenna
firir austan borg,
vígspiǫll vaka,
– þat mun viti kallaðr.
Mun herr koma
hinig af bragði
ok brenna bœ
firir buðlungi.

‘I can see fire blazing
east of the fortress,
war-news wakening,
– a warning beacon that will mean.
Soldiery will come
in sudden speed towards us
and burn the palace
in despite of the prince.

20 ‘Munat þú halda
Hleiðrar stóli,
rauðum hringum
né regingrióti.
Tǫkum á mǫndli,
mær, skarpara –
eruma va*ml*ar
í valdreyra.

‘You will not hold
the throne of Hleiðr,
the gold-red rings
nor the grindstone of power.
Let us grasp the mill-handle,
girl, more keenly –
we are not squeamish
in the gore of slaughter.

21 ‘Mól míns fǫður
mær ramliga,
þvíat hón feigð fira
fiǫlmargra sá.’

‘My father’s girl
ground lustily,
for she saw the near death
of numberless men.’

18/1 hǫndla] hǫlða SR, holda T 18/3 ÷T 18/5 Vaki] ɪc SR 18/6 vill hlýða] *so* T, hlyþa vill SR 19/4 mun] mō T 19/5 Mun] Mō T 19/5 herr] h^{er} T 19/6 hinig af] hung a T 19/7 bœ] bæ SR, bǒ T 20/1 Munat þú] Mun̄ aðr T 20/3 hringum] ringō T 20/4 -grióti] g^{ri}ote T 20/5 Tǫkum] ᴍc SR 20/5 mǫndli] mundli T (*cf. Mundilfœri, Vafþrúðnismál 23/1*) 20/7 vamlar] valmar SR, *with small subsript stroke between* l *and* m, valn^{ar} T 21/2 ramliga] rangliga T 21/3 þvíat] þt SR 21/4 fiǫlmargra sá] fiolð of vissi T

Stukku stórar
st[ø]ðr frá lúðri,
iárn[*i v*]arðar:
'Mǫlum enn framarr!'

Off burst the massive
mainstays from the mill-crib,
girded with iron:
'Let us grind even further!'

22 'Mǫlum enn framarr:
mon Yrsu sonr
víg[s] Hálfdana[r]
hefna [á] Fróða.
Sá mun hennar
heitinn verða
burr ok bróðir –
vitum báðar þa[*t*].'

'Let us grind even further:
Yrsa's son will
for Hálfdan's slaughter
take vengeance on Fróði.
He will come
to be called
her son and brother –
both of us know that.'

23 Mólu meyiar,
megins k[*o*]stuðu –
vóru ungar
í iǫtunmóði.
Skulfu skap[t]tré,
skautz lúðr ofan,
hraut hinn hǫfgi
hallr sundr í tvau.

The girls ground on,
gave proof of their strength –
those young ones were
in giant wrath.
The timber frames shuddered,
the mill-crib shot to the ground,
the cumbrous stone
cracked in two.

24 En bergrisa
brúðr orð um kvað:
'Malit hǫfum, Fróði,
sem munum hætta.
Hafa fullstaðit
flióð at meldri.'

And the crag-giants'
consort had her say:
'We have milled so, Fróði,
that we shall mill no more.
They have stood long enough,
these ladies, at the milling.'

21/5 stukku] stu^{c}o T 21/6 støðr] *so* T (stǒðr), steðr SR 21/7 iárni varðar] *so* T, iarnar fiarþar SR 22/3 vígs] v^{ið} SR, T 22/3 Hálfdanar] halfdana SR, T 22/4 á] ÷ SR, T 22/5 mun] mō T 22/8 báðar] baðịṛ *corrected to* bað^{ar} T 22/8 þat] *so* T, þar SR 23/2 kostuðu] *so* T, kɔstvðv (*i.e.* '*flung*') SR 23/3 vóru] oro T 23/5 skulfu] ıc SR (*but preceded by* ⁝), T 23/5 skapttré] skaptre SR, scaftre T 23/6 skautz] scauz T 23/7 hinn] iñ T 23/8 tvau] tau T 24/3 hǫfum Fróði] heui ec f^{yrir} m^{ik} T (*cf. 17/3*) 24/4 sem] s̄m 24/4 munum] monū T

Commentary

Prose The setting for the acquisition of the giantesses, on a visit by Fróði to Fjǫlnir in Sweden, has probably been surmised by Snorri on the basis of the poem's description of the girls' feats in Sweden, along with the tradition of visits between Fróði and Fjǫlnir found already in *Ynglingatal* 1 (*Skj* B I, 7). The quernstones on the other hand were found in Denmark, according to Snorri. Whilst it is possible to construct a scenario in which the giantesses come from Jǫtunheimar via Sweden to Denmark, it is more likely that a mixing of traditions occurs here; the poem at least gives no provenance for either the girls or the stones, merely noting that the girls were responsible for the stones' appearance. The poem also indicates that the stones rolled through the realm of giants, into the hands of men, who took them. Snorri's account of one Hengikjǫptr presenting them to Fróði is thus also inconsistent with the poem. Hengikjǫptr is either a giant (cf. *Hengjankjapta*, a giantess in a verse of Þorbjǫrn dísarskáld, cited by Snorri in *Skáldskaparmál* ch. 4: *SnE* 97; ed. Faulkes I, 17; trans. Faulkes 74) – which seems contextually unlikely – or a *heiti* ('hanging chin', in reference to his beard) for Óðinn (found in *þulur* jj 4, *Skj* B I, 673, as *hengikeptr*). An ill-fated gift presented by a disguised Óðinn would be in character, and Snorri is likely to have invented this aspect of the story. Snorri's summary follows the poem fairly closely up to the point where vengeance is wrought on Fróði. The poem makes no mention of Mýsingr, unless in some lost section. Mýsingr does appear as the overthrower of Fróði in *Skjǫldunga saga*, however, though he is not a sea-king there. In *þulur* a 3 (*Skj* B I, 658), Mýsingr is listed as a sea-king: if this antedates Snorri, he could have used the ascription to help produce the story he gives. He would have been aided by the existence of a tradition such as is found in Saxo, that Fróði was killed by a beast from the sea (albeit a female one), which has ancient mythological parallels. The rest of the tale of Grotti, that it was taken by Mýsingr along with Fenja and Menja, and told to grind salt, ending up in the deep still grinding, is an aetiological folktale found in Norway and Iceland, and elsewhere, which has nothing to do with the poem *Grottasǫngr*: the famous mill Grotti may, however, have been associated with this tale already by Snorri's time, especially as Snæbjǫrn's verse implies a tradition in which Grotti ended up in the sea.

1 The first *helmingr* is spoken by the two giant maids in SR and T; in C the third person is used. Whilst the C form is perhaps more logical, it lacks the dramatic force gained by the use of direct speech here, and is probably a rationalisation on the part of Snorri (C, citing merely an excerpt, is likely to represent the form of text closest to Snorri's original here) to accommodate the stanza to its context more readily as a straightforward quotation.

The first stanza sets out the scene and the characters. The two girls are Fenja and Menja; they are strong – hence their usefulness – but they are also gifted with foresight (in common with many giants: cf. Vafþrúðnir (*Vafþrúðnismál* 44)). The irony that this foresight had failed to prevent their enslavement is not considered; the focus is upon the use they will make of this foresight against Fróði, and their enslavement is regarded (perhaps disingenuously) as a deliberate act of self-humiliation to achieve their final goal. The mill, with its connotations of turning fortune, will be the means of their grinding out misfortune for the ill-treatment they receive at the king's hands. Hence the explanation in st. 10 of how, with foreknowledge, they had arranged the discovery of the quernstones and their own enslavement (presumably the same implication lies in the repetition of *framvísar tvær* in st. 13: they are prescient in entering the battle in which, it may be surmised, they were caught and enslaved). Their bondage at the mill is their means of power over the king. Naturally, this may be felt by the reader as something of a justification after the event – they had milled wealth for the king happily enough to start with, after all, but it is a claim the girls themselves seem keen to defend.

Fróði is identified as son of Friðleifr. This must originally have identified him clearly as frið-Fróði, not as the semi-historical king of the fifth century, but several of the Fróðis of the Norse genealogies are sons of Friðleifr (see the family trees in the Introduction): clearly confusion between the mythical and the historical Fróðis had a long tradition. Although Snorri identified the Fróði of *Grottasǫngr* as the peace-Fróði, it is not clear that the poet intended more than the vaguest revelation of his identity by calling him son of Friðleifr.

1/3 *framvísar* occurs in the late *Grípisspá* 21/7, and in a verse of Bjǫrn Hítdœlakappi (*framvísar dísir*, *Skj* B I, 282, dated to 1024), and in a verse in *Hjálmþérs saga ok Ǫlvers* ch. 14.

1/4 Fenja may derive from *fen*, 'deep pool', and Menja from *men*, 'necklace, jewellery' (de Vries 1977 regards *man* as a more likely source, i.e. 'slave-girl'). In the poem Menja speaks mainly of the treasures they are to grind out for Fróði. Fenja's name would be a generic giant-name, 'dweller in the fens, pools', but this underwater home would confer powers of prophecy (as with Frigg: *ørlǫg Frigg hygg ek at ǫll viti*, 'of all fates Frigg has, I think, full knowledge', as *Lokasenna* 29 says; Frigg's home was Fensalir (*Vǫluspá* 33/6): see *PE* II, commentary to *Vǫluspá* 20/3, 33/6 and *Lokasenna* 21/4–6, as well as *Grímnismál* 7): Fenja's chief role is to prophesy the end of Fróði. The other implication of *fen* is treasure: cf. the kennings *fenglóð*, *fenlogi* for 'gold' (*Plácítusdrápa* 55, Skj B I, 621; verse from *Ǫrvar-Odds saga*, VII.9, *Skj* B II, 318). (Other possible etymologies are listed in de Vries 1977, *s.v. Fenja*.)

1/5 Fróði means 'wise', but also 'virile, fecund' (see *PE* II, commentary to *Skírnismál* 1/5); it is the latter sense that must have been to the fore in the name of peace-Fróði, the bestower of *ár ok friðr*, 'abundance and peace', but probably the former sense was more important in the names of historical men such as the king of the Heathobards.

1/8 *man*, 'slave-girl', is here used in a collective sense.

1/8 *hafðar* SR, T, *giǫrvar* C. It is possible to derive both manuscript forms from one written original ('gervar' being more likely than 'hafðar'), but *giǫrvar* may be a sense replacement by the C scribe, *gera at* and *hafa at* both meaning 'put to use'.

2/1 On the sense of *lúðr*, 'mill-crib', see the Introduction II.
2/3 The word *griá* occurs in Old Norse only here and in 10/2. It is possible, given the defective state of the text from which our manuscripts were copied, that 'gria' is a corrupt form, but what it could be derived from is not obvious. To read it as a corrupt form of *grá*, 'grey' – the most obvious solution – is scarcely satisfactory, as there is no obvious reason for such a common word to be corrupted twice, other than the initial *grj-* of *grjóts* preceding it; 'grey' is moreover a vacuous description of the rock (though this cannot wholly preclude its appearance in the poem). If we are to seek a more satisfactory interpretation, the word must clearly refer to some type of rock, perhaps one particularly suitable for quernstones (German volcanic rock was the best available, and was sometimes imported into Scandinavia; see Curwen 1937, and *KLNM*, *s.v. kvarn*, but the narrative of the poem implies the stones were derived from local mountains). The suggestion of *LP* is the most likely, that *griá* is accusative plural in 2/3, and genitive plural in 10/2, and is derived from a nominative *gré*; de Vries (1977, *s.v. *gré*) suggests a possible etymology from a root *greu-*, 'feinreiben'. Thus *griótz griá* would mean 'grindstones of rock'.
2/6 *ynði* is probably meant in the more concrete sense of 'refreshment' rather than the usual 'delight' (cf. *Vǫluspá* 61/8, where there is a hint of 'liquid refreshment').
2/7 This line is problematic: whilst the general sense that Fróði told the girls to get straight on with work is clear, it is not obvious whether Fróði made his promise of rest once they had started work, or whether he made no mention of it at all. Once the noise of the mill starts, Fróði again tells the girls to work (3/5–6). St. 7 seems to indicate that he said nothing further to them until he told them they could have no rest, after which their goodwill towards him disappears. Yet st. 4–6 seem to show the girls' good disposition towards the king, which would readily be motivated by the promise of rest mentioned in st. 2; their violent reaction after st. 7 would moreover follow all the more naturally if it was a result of Fróði breaking his word. On the whole, however, it seems most likely that no promise was made. St. 2 then demonstrates Fróði's importunate nature: he cannot wait to get at the mill's gold, and has no regard for his servants. That is the limit of his character; breaking of promises lies beyond this narrow scope.
2/8 *hlióm* is a word applied in particular to music (singing or instrumental); it thus looks forward to the girls' song, but probably also encompasses the harmonic whirring of the mill. The word is also used in kennings for 'battle' (*LP*, *s.v. hljómr*); possibly the poet intended to hint at the violence to be milled out for Fróði.

3/1–2 These lines, unfortunately absent from T, present some problems. The seemingly nonsensical manuscript 'þulu' (nonetheless retained by Faulkes (ed. I, 53; trans. 108) and interpreted as 'caused to be uttered') must be a mistake for 'þutu' (cf. the *kvern þjótandi*, 'whirring quern', of *Hlǫðskviða* 8); the manuscript 'þæḡ horviɴar' appears to be feminine genitive singular, without any referent. It has been construed as referring to the quern, the thing from which silence has been banished, but this is syntactically difficult given that no noun is present to which 'silence-banished' would refer. The slight emendation adopted here makes the word a feminine nominative plural, in agreement with the subject of the sentence, namely the slave-girls, who, as they set to work, are 'shunned by silence'. A further possibility would be to emend to *þǫgn horfin var*, 'silence was banished' (Kock 1923–35, §69). The word *þǫgn* refers to lack of speech, not just absence of sound: the next two lines show the girls busily telling each other what to do, and soon will follow their singing. This is the *hlióm* referred to in 2/8. The unusual formation *þǫgnhorfinn* may be intended to recall the expression *heillum horfinn*, 'shunned by fortune'.

3/3 *leggium* is to be understood as a jussive subjunctive. The manuscripts consistently use the first person plural indicative form in place of the earlier subjunctive (which was beginning to disappear already in the earliest records, and had been completely superseded by 1500; Noreen 1970, §536.2); the earlier forms would have been *leggim*; *léttim* (3/4); *malim* (5/1,2, 21/8, 22/1); *takim* (20/5).

3/3 The mechanics of the action described here are unclear. *Leggja* would most naturally be taken in the sense 'set up', but it is clear from 2/2 that the mill is already set up. Some preparation of the corn-bin in the way of cleaning might be expected, but this would hardly be described as *leggja*. The mill should have been firmly fixed (for example to a wall), but perhaps some extra strengthening precautions are taken by the giantesses here. Also unusual is the use of *lúðra* in the plural; the mill could only have one corn-bin, though it might be seen as having two halves on either side of the stones. Lüning's view, that the girls are proposing to stop milling (see von See et al. 2000, 880), seems unlikely given the stage of proceedings at this point in the poem.

3/4 The girls lighten the stones, that is, they adjust the upper stone by raising the lightening tree. This would no doubt reduce the *þyt*, 'noise', of 3/1 to a more acceptable level. The reading of T is a misinterpretation of minims ('steuiū' for 'steinū'), but the resulting *stefium*, 'refrains', may have been connected in the mind of the T scribe with the slave-girls' singing.

4/2 *snúðga* is probably a weak adjective, but it could also be taken as a compound adjective (cf. *hvítaauri* in *Vǫluspá* 19/4; see commentary in *PE* II). The *snúðgasteinn* would be the top stone of the quern, which whirled around over the motionless lower stone (designated possibly by the *hǫfga halli* of 12/7). For the adjective *snúðigr* cf. Bjǫrn krepphendi, *Magnússdrápa* 9/4 (*Skj* B I, 406), where it describes a flying weapon-shaft.

4/3–4 Whilst these lines emphasise the unceasing labour of the giant maidens, working on whilst the rest of the servants slept, they also hint at a magical enchantment wrought by the whirring mill, though this is not a theme developed in the extant form of the poem. A sleep enchantment forms an important part of the myth of the *sampo* in Finnish (see Introduction V).

4/5 If Menja's name derives from *men*, 'necklace, treasure', it is appropriate that she should be the one to speak of the riches they are to mill out.

4/6 *meldrar*: SR 'meldr', T 'meldrs' point to an antecedent 'meldr', corrected in T; 'meldr' would be badly copied from 'meldr[ar]' omitting the superscript abbre-

viation for *-ar* (more likely than the omission of 's' in a supposed **meldrs*).
4/6 *komit*: the manuscripts read 'kom̄' (SR), 'comī' (T), i.e. *komin*, which would mean 'Menja had come to the milling'. But she must be included in the *þær* of 3/1: she has been fully involved in the milling process already. The small emendation adopted here changes the sense, so that the poet is saying the milling had reached the point where the flour starts to emerge from between the quernstones (*meldr* outside *Grottasǫngr* appears always to mean 'result of the milling process, flour', but here a sense 'milling process' is implied; see von See et al. 2000, 883). This prompts Menja to speak of the riches they are to mill out in place of the expected wheat-flour.

5/1 Although *mǫlum* is probably jussive, standing for an earlier *malim*, it could be indicative: Menja could be simply pointing out the nature of the *meldr* as it emerges from the mill.
5/2 *mǫlum alsælan* is a difficult construction. *Alsælan* must be an accusative masculine adjective (cf. parallel compounds such as *matsæll*, 'fortunate in respect to food', a nickname in *Bandamanna saga* ch. 10), agreeing with an understood *Fróða*, 'let us grind Fróði happy in all things', but *mala* is not elsewhere recorded with an adjective used as an object in this way. Snorri, in his prose rendering, substitutes the noun *sælu*. There does not appear to be any abstract noun from which *alsælan* could be derived or corrupted, however; Snorri has merely simplified. *Alsæll* appears to be used primarily in Christian religious contexts: *alsælan hug* occurs in *Heilagra anda vísur* 11/4 (*Skj* B II, 178), and the word is also used in the Stockholm Homily Book 29/31 (SG).
5/4 *feginslúðri*: for the use of a genitive adjective as the first element in a compound cf. *Skírnismál* 26/1: *tamsvendi* (and commentary in *PE* II).
5/5–8 It is possible that this *helmingr* is based on actual charms (von See et al. 2000, 886): cf. the phrase *sem á dúni søfr dóttir Atla*, 'where Atli's daughter sleeps on down', in the inscription from Årdal kirke, Sogn (Olsen 1941–60, IV, 126–36).

6 This stanza seems to be a deliberate reflection of the traditional description of the *Fróða friðr*; this well-known time of peace and prosperity, described in the Introduction V, 'King Fróði', is thus attributed to the working of the mill (such a clear, or exclusive, connection was not made elsewhere). The poet makes no allusion, however, to the tale of the gold ring remaining undisturbed for many years beside the highway on Jalangrsheiðr. It is likely that the poet has made use of *Skjǫldunga saga* or a closely related source in this deliberately allusive stanza – though the lateness of the Latin recension of *Skjǫldunga saga* admits the remote possibility that it may itself have been influenced by *Grottasǫngr*.

The phrases used have an air of legal terminology, but exact parallels cannot in fact be found. *Sitt bjó til betra* occurs in a verse of Ámundi Árnason (thirteenth century) describing a ruler, a true friend of the law and righteousness (*Skj* B II, 59), where the sense appears to be 'prepared himself for a better [home]' in a religious sense. The use of *búa* in an absolute sense, 'prepare', 'work', without a reflexive ('prepare oneself') or a direct object is unusual, but cf. *Rígsþula* 16/4: *bió til váðar*, 'prepared to make cloth'; the construction is presumably intended to

parallel *til bana orka* of the next line. *Búumk til vígs*, 'I am ready for battle', occurs in Egill's *lausavísa* 29 (*Skj* B I, 49). The nearest parallel to *orka til bana* seems to be *orka til þarfa* in *lausavísa* 43 of Egill (*Skj* B I, 52), meaning effectively 'help'.
6/5 Compare *Grípisspá* 15/5–6: *þú munt hǫggva hvǫsso sverði*, 'you will strike with sharp sword'.
6/7 *bana bróður*: the brother's killer is an ancient mythical motif (see *Lokasenna* 17/6 and commentary in *PE* II), here placed in a heroic context and given legal rather than mythological import (cf. the *bróður bani* of *Sigrdrífumál* 35).

7 It is possible that some lines are missing at the beginning of the stanza, though the continuity of sense in the extant text can be defended: the slave-girls' effusion on Fróði's behalf is met with the cold indifference of his command to take no rest.
7/1–2 Compare *Oddrúnargrátr* 8, *svá at hón ekki kvað orð it fyrra*, 'for she had spoken no word before'. Here and at 18/6 the metrically better T text is preferred to the text of SR (*kvað ekki*, *hlýða vill*). However, given the lack of metrical regularity elsewhere in the poem (e.g. 15/1–2), the T reading does not necessarily represent the poet's intention.
7/3–4 The manuscripts read *sofið eigi þit né of sal gaukar*, which makes little sense. Clearly a corrupt text lies behind both T and SR. Apart from the grammatical problems it may also be noted that cuckoos do not frequent halls (SG). The emendation is based on Snorri's prose account; he says *þá gaf hann þeim eigi lengri hvíld eða svefn en gaukrinn þagði eða lióð mátti kveða*, 'he gave them no more rest or sleep than a cuckoo is silent or it takes to sing a song'. The phrase *syngrat gaukr* occurs in Egill's *lausavísa* 27 (*Skj* B I, 48) – 'the cuckoo does not sing' when the hound is circling below it; both poetic contexts appear to allude to the cuckoo as an archetypal incessant chatterer (other associations of the cuckoo in ancient Norse and Old English sources, either with magic, as in some runic bracteates (see McKinnell, Simek and Düwel 2004, 72–3), or as a bird of ill-omen (e.g. the Old English *Seafarer* 53), seem irrelevant). Egill's is the only other use of *gaukr* recorded in verse in *LP*; that the poet of *Grottasǫngr* has borrowed from Egill is indicated moreover by the occurrence in the same stanza of Egill of the word *sjǫtul*, the only other occurrence of which is in *Grottasǫngr* 16/7. (Egill's verse reads: *þar nautk enn sem optarr arnstalls sjǫtul-bjarnar*, 'there I benefited again, as often, from the settle of an eagle's pedestal *bjǫrn*'; the pedestal that eagles settle on is a rock, equivalent to *arinn*, 'hearth-stone': hence Arinbjǫrn, Egill's comrade.) It appears that various scribal misreadings of letters and abbreviations have taken place to produce the text of these lines as found in the manuscripts; at least one, misreading of 't' as 'l', occurs elsewhere (cf. 3/1 *þutu*). Another possibility would be to allow the manuscript reading to stand, and assume some lines have dropped out, so that the statement would have been to the effect 'Sleep no [more than x's do not sing] nor the cuckoos about the hall', but Snorri's summary does not reveal anything these lines could have contained.
7/6 The sort of *ljóð* implied here is the short charm of the sort listed in *Hávamál* 146–63, suitable for any eventuality; particularly swift must have been the *ljóð* against a speeding weapon (*Hávamál* 150).

8/1 The form 'varattv' in SR is probably a slip. Noreen (1970, §534.2.d) cites the loss of *-t* in the second person singular preterite when *þú* follows immediately; here however a negative *-a-* intervenes. Since the negative *a* was archaic by the time of the manuscript, *varattu* could possibly represent an erroneously reconstructed form. Note that the form *kvaðattu* occurs in *Oddrúnargrátr* 12/5.
8/2 *fullspakr*: the link between wisdom and prescience emerges clearly in *Vǫluspá* 29/3: *spaklig* (see commentary ad loc.). Fróði is 'the wise' (*a multarum rerum scientia sic dictus*, 'so called from his knowledge of many matters', as *Skjǫldunga saga* puts it), but he lacked foresight for himself, unlike the giant maidens (or so they claim).
8/3 *málvinr*: lit. 'a friend in speech'. The word is used with deep irony: Fróði was far from friendly in his speech to the girls. The word is elsewhere used in the sense of 'sweetheart' (*Guðrúnarkviða I* 20, *Krákumál* 20): the 'people's sweetheart' refers to Fróði's popularity as bestower of peace and well-being. Menja uses the title with biting sarcasm.

9 Five mighty giants, four of them named, are mentioned to impress upon Fróði that he has taken on more than he bargained for in buying the girls. Hrungnir's father appears to be an invention of the poet of *Grottasǫngr*; he is nowhere else mentioned.

The story of Hrungnir, 'Noisy' (de Vries 1977, *s.v.*), is recounted in *Skáldskaparmál* ch. 17 (*SnE* 100–4; ed. Faulkes I, 20–2; trans. Faulkes 77–9), based on *Haustlǫng* 14–19 (*Skj* B I, 17–18); he is also mentioned in *Hárbarðsljóð* 15, *Lokasenna* 61, 63, *Hymiskviða* 16, *Sigrdrífumál* 15, *Ragnarsdrápa* 17 (*Skj* B I, 4), Kormakr's *lausavísa* 14 (*Skj* B I, 73), and *Háttatal* 30 (*Skj* B II, 69). In a contest with Þórr, Hrungnir defended himself by placing his shield beneath him, believing the god would attack from below; he cast a whetstone at Þórr, who shattered it in mid-air, but received a splinter of it in his forehead; the god crushed the stone head of Hrungnir.

Þjazi (meaning obscure, but probably originally related to 'father' words: de Vries 1977, *s.v.*) was the father of Skaði, wife of Njǫrðr (*Skáldskaparmál* ch. G56: *SnE* 30; ed. Faulkes I, 1–3; trans. Faulkes 59–61); Þjazi abducted Iðunn from Ásgarðr by assuming the form of an eagle; Loki retrieved Iðunn, and Þjazi pursued; when he reached Ásgarðr, the Æsir set fire to his feathers and slew him. His daughter marched off to Ásgarðr in panoply of war to seek vengeance, but was placated by the promise of one of the gods as husband, the condition being she had to choose him by his feet alone (*Skáldskaparmál* ch. G56: *SnE* 80–1; ed. Faulkes I, 2; trans Faulkes 61). Þjazi is also mentioned in *Haustlǫng* 1 (*Skj* B I, 14), Kormakr's *Sigurðardrápa* 6/4 (*Skj* B I, 69), *Grímnismál* 11, *Hárbarðsljóð* 19, *Lokasenna* 50, 51, and *Hyndluljóð* 30.

Iði, 'Industrious' (de Vries 1977, *s.v.*), was brother of Þjazi (*Skáldskaparmál* ch. G56: *SnE* 81; ed. Faulkes I, 3; trans. Faulkes 61); when their father died, his sons divided their inheritance by each taking a mouthful of gold. The name also occurs in *Bjarkamál* 5 (*Skj* B I, 171), *Þórsdrápa* 2 (*Skj* B I, 139), *Friðþjófs rímur* I, 21/3 (*Rímnasafn* I, 414), in two anonymous verses (*Skj* B I, 601, 604), and in *þulur* (*Skj* B I, 658 st. 1/4).

Aurnir (probably 'Muddy': *aur-* is a common element in giant names; cf. Aurboða, Aurgelmir, Aurgrímnir) occurs as a giant name in *þulur* (*Skj* B I, 659 b 4); in Sturla Þórðarson's *Hákonarkviða* 19 (1263–4, *Skj* B II, 122); and in a verse from *Bergbúaþáttr* 9 (*Skj* B II, 228). It also occurs in a context at least comparable with *Grottasǫngr*, in the third of three *vísur* found in *Hemings þáttr* (from Hauksbók) sung by a troll-woman flying through the air on a wolf, carrying a trough of blood and limbs and prophesying defeat for Haraldr harðráði as he lies off the coast at Scarborough (*Skj* B I, 400; recent edition and discussion in Poole 1991, 16–17). The troll-woman is called *brúðr Aurnis jóða*, 'bride of the children of Aurnir'. Nothing is known of the history of Aurnir.

9/7 *bergrisa*: the word is not found elsewhere in Eddic poetry; it is used in a tenth-century verse (*Skj* B I, 172 st. 7), in *Buslubœn* 8 (*Skj* B II, 352; *Bósa saga* ch. 5), and also in *Gylfaginning* ch. 15, 21, 27 (*SnE* 23, 29, 33; ed. Faulkes 18, 23, 25; trans. Faulkes 18, 22, 25).

9/7–8 Cf. *Oddrúnargrátr* 11: *sem við brœðrom tveim of borin værim*, 'as if we were born of two brothers'.

9/8 The alliteration falls on the second stressed syllable.

10/1 *Grotti* is the 'grinder'; *grotti* survives in Norn and Faeroese as a designation for the nave in the lower quernstone, and in Norwegian for the block in the nave; in Danish dialect the verb *grotte* means 'grind up fine' (see de Vries 1977 on the etymology).

10/2 See commentary to 2/3.

10/7–8 SG retain the manuscript reading *ef vissi vitt* (T *vit*) *vætr til hennar*, taking this to mean 'if sorcery did not belong to her'. However, the mention of magic here appears inappropriate: it is not a theme developed in the poem, and even if it were, the statement by the girl that she would not be working the mill if she – or it – were not in possession of magic powers would be pointless in the context. Moreover, the word rendered 'magic' – *vitt* or variants – is found exceedingly rarely, occurring with any certainty only in a couple of passages in the Norwegian laws and probably in the archaic *Ynglingatal* 6 (see Cleasby and Vigfusson 1957, *s.v. vitt*, for citations), where it most likely refers not to mere 'magic', but to a particular (and now unidentifiable) object used in conjury. Rather, the stanza in fact must relate to, and justify, the girls' attribute of foreknowledge: they are stating that they knew about the situation they now find themselves in long before it actually took place; therefore they allowed it to happen, with the result that they now command control over the mill, with which they will work a punishment for Fróði (as noted, this may be more their *post factum* explanation for their plight). The emendations adopted here are fairly minor: final *-m* is regularly dropped before a labial in the manuscripts (cf. *stóðu[m]*, next stanza; see Noreen 1970, §531.3), double and single consonants alternate often without regard to phonology (and *tt* here is represented merely by a dotted t); the change of *hennar* to *kvernar* is more major. *Hennar* makes no sense, as it cannot meaningfully be related to any antecedent; it is also suspect semantically as a weak word coming at the climax of the forcefully stated stanza. *Kvernar* is the most apposite word to fit the context from which *hennar* could be corrupted.

11 Eiríkr Magnússon suggests the image of stones being hurled by giantesses may be related to the account of Rymbegla: *Þat var á einu ári, þá er Fróði var gamall, at reiðar þrumur kómu stórar ok eldingar; þá hvarf sól af himni ok skálf jǫrð svá at bjǫrg hrutu ór stað ok þá kómu bjǫrg ór jǫrðu ok viltusk allir spádómar*, 'It was one year, when Fróði was old, that mighty wild thunderings and lightnings came; then the sun disappeared from the sky and the earth shook so that the mountains quivered from their place and crags came out of the earth and all forecasts went awry'. This is based on *Skjǫldunga saga*, of which the Latin summary here reads (ch. 3, ÍF 35, 6): *Deinde post multorum annorum curriculum insveta facta ecclipsis solis cum terræ motu saxa et scopulos loco movente atqve disrumpente. Illum igitur putant fuisse annum et tempus passionis Christi*, 'Then after the course of many years there occurred an unwonted eclipse of the sun and an earthquake, in which rocks and crags were dislodged and cast down. It is believed that this occurred in the year and at the time of the passion of Christ'. It is difficult to say if the motif of the age of peace and wealth ending in natural cataclysms is older than this Christian version, but it may well be. The difficulty with associating the emergence of the millstones with such events is that this would scarcely allow enough time for the construction of the mill and acquisition of the slave-girls to work it: the cataclysms mark the end of Fróði's reign, not merely an event within it. The poem does not present the casting up of the stones as an apocalyptic event, and the collapse of the mill cannot be equated with such natural events as *Skjǫldunga saga* describes. On the whole, therefore, it is difficult to see any particular connection with *Skjǫldunga saga* at this point.

11/1 The use of *vér* (plural) in place of the dual *vit* may be a scribal slip.

11/4 *firir iǫrð neðan* characterises the giantesses as chthonic or underworld beings: the phrase is used in *Lokasenna* 23, *Vǫluspá* 42 and *Alvíssmál* 3, all relating to giants, dwarfs or the dead.

11/6 *meginverkum* is otherwise found only in *Heilagra anda vísur* (*Skj* B II, 178). Von See et al. (2000, 909) suggest it is borrowed from Old English *mægenweorc*, and cite the *Paris Psalter*, Psalm 91/4.

11/7 SR has 'færþv̄'; the T reading 'haufō' probably represents a misinterpretation of 'hofō', i.e. *hófom*, 'lifted'; this may well be the original reading, which SR has replaced with the semantic equivalent *færðum*; SG quote some parallels (an Uppland runic inscription, and *Þjalar Jóns saga*) where *fœra steinn* (*bjǫrg*) *ór stað* is used of moving stones. This is the only place in the poem where *œ* is represented by the up-to-date 'æ' in SR (except once in the commonplace word *bœ*); the T reading is preferred as being marginally more likely to be earlier.

11/8 *setberg*: a saddle-backed mountain, suitable for seating giants (SG); the word occurs in topographical names in Norway and Iceland (Fritzner 1886–1972, *s.v.*; Kålund 1908–18, I 428, II 390), as well as Norse-colonised areas of England (Watts 2004, *s.v. Sadberge*, *Sedbergh*), where such mountains may have been associated with gods as well as giants (see Ælfric, *De falsis diis* 138, in Pope 1969, 684): this would lend a more aggressive tone to the statement, with the giantesses appearing in a traditional role as antagonists of the gods. The word occurs twice in kennings: *setbergs bǫnd*, 'gods of the mountain', i.e. giants, in Eilífr Guðrúnarson (*Skj* B I, 144) (though Weber 1970 questions this interpretation), and *linna setberg*, 'mountain seat of serpents', i.e. gold, in

Eyjólfr dáðaskáld's *Bandadrápa* 3 (*Skj* B I, 191). In *Gylfaginning* ch. 47 (*SnE* 59; ed. Faulkes 43; trans. Faulkes 45 as 'table mountain') the giant Skrýmir thrusts a *setberg* in front of him to defend himself against Þórr; possibly the poet of *Grottasǫngr* is alluding to the lost Eddic lay that Snorri almost certainly used as a source (see Brennecke 1981).

12/5–6 The same words are used to describe the dislodging of the stones from the earth as are used in st. 4 for the action of turning the quern made from these rocks. The *snúðgi steinn* and the *hǫfgi hallr* (or *snúðgasteinn* and *hǫfgahallr*) may designate the two stones used to make the quern, as Snorri seems to have understood (*fannz í Danmǫrk kvernsteinar tveir*, 'two quernstones were found in Denmark'); see commentary to 4/2.

13–14 The exploits of the giant girls in Sweden must relate in some way to Fróði. It was presumably through defeat in a Swedish war that the girls fell into Fróði's hands as captives. Snorri appears to have connected this with frið-Fróði, who is said to have purchased the girls while visiting Fjǫlnir of Sweden. However, in *Skjǫldunga saga* it is Frodo IV, son of Fridleifus, and father of Ingialldus (and thus in origin the Heathobard king), who has the greatest connection with Sweden. Frodo's half-brother Alo, a pirate, was adopted as king of Sweden, upon which Frodo decided to assassinate him in case he should come seeking his patrimony in Denmark. This task was entrusted to Starcardus, who slew the king in his bath. Frodo then defeated the Swedish king Iorundus and took his daughter. Iorundus murdered Frodo as he was making a night sacrifice. Further exploits of this Fróði are recounted in *Ynglinga saga* ch. 26; he attacks and lays waste Sweden after King Óttarr has refused to pay tribute; Óttarr in turn attacks Denmark while Fróði is absent. It is more likely that the poet of *Grottasǫngr* wished to evoke these Swedish wars to accommodate the giantesses into an accepted 'historical' tradition, rather than the weaker links between frið-Fróði and Sweden. However, the two leaders mentioned, Gotþormr and Knúi, are not found associated with any Fróði elsewhere. Gotþormr is a name known from the Sigurðr poems as a brother of Gunnarr, Hǫgni, and Guðrún (*Grípisspá* 50, *Brot* 4, *Sigurðarkviða in skamma* 20, 22, *Guðrúnarkviða II* 7, *Hyndluljóð* 27). The name Knúi is found in a list of heroic names in *Ǫrvar-Odds saga*, where Guttormr also occurs (*Skj* B II, 316 IV 3, 5).

There appears little justification for the giantesses' engagement in the wars mentioned in terms of the structure of the poem. The poet may be intending to imitate *Darraðarljóð*, where the engagement in war by the weaving valkyries as they proclaim the outcome of the battle is essential. There is also some similarity to the part played by Þorgerðr hǫlgabrúðr and her sister Irpa in Hákon jarl's battle with the Jómsvíkingar (in *Óláfs saga Tryggvasonar*, ch. 154–5, in *Flateyjarbók* I, 210–11).The *Grottasǫngr* poet may have wished to appropriate some of the terror of these beings for his giantesses.

13/4 *í fólk stigum*: cf. *í fólk ganga*, *lausavísa* 2 of Óláfr inn helgi (*Skj* B I, 210) and *í fólk vaða* of *Darraðarljóð* 4 (all meaning 'to engage in war').

13/5 *beittum biǫrnu*: it is difficult to decide between the nearly homophonous T and SR forms *beittum/beiddum biǫrnu*, both with the general meaning 'we hunted bears', but *beita*, 'make bite, bait', better emphasises the heroic risks the girls undertake (cf. *Qlkofra þáttr* ch. 1, ÍF 11, 86, where Qlkofri, having got into trouble for accidentally burning down a group of chieftains' woodlands, is refused help by his former patrons, who declare *at þeir mundu eigi þeim birni beitask*, 'that they would not bait that bear', i.e. bring trouble upon themselves). The image of warriors as bears being overpowered as an example of heroic feats is found in *Helgakviða Hundingsbana II* 8/5: *er ek biqrno tók í Bragalundi*, 'when I took bears in Bragalundr', which may have influenced *Grottasqngr*. *Bjqrn*, 'bear', used in the sense of 'warrior' seems to occur only in riddling or enigmatic contexts (thus in the example just cited, Helgi is attempting to be evasive, being uncertain who he is talking to; for other examples see von See et al. 2000, 913–14), but the riddling context appears to be lost on the poet of *Grottasqngr*. Bugge suggests an emendation (adopted by SG) to *sneiddum brynjur*; it is based on *Víkarsbálkr* 11/7–8 (*Skj* B II, 346): *brynjur sníddum ok brutum skjqldu*, 'we sliced byrnies and shattered shields', which might then be viewed as a likely borrowing from *Grottasqngr*. The word-order *brynjur sneiddum* would be metrically preferable, as in *Víkarsbálkr*. However, the emendation appears too far removed from the forms of SR and T to be adopted here.

13/8 *gráserkiat*: the warriors are 'grey-shirted' with iron mail-shirts; cf. *hringserkjat lið*, 'ring-shirted army', in *Merlínusspá* II, 46 (*Skj* B II, 33); *í grám serkjum*, 'in grey shirts', in *Qrvar-Odds saga* (*Skj* B II, 311, III 3/3).

13/8 SR 'lit' is a result of hypercorrection of final -ð to a (supposed) earlier -t.

14 An interference in politics is found also in *Atlamál* 96–9, where Guðrún and her brothers go roving, killing a king and freeing outlaws. This is similar in that a woman is involved in these Viking activities, and in the contrast which both poems draw between the former life of freedom and the present one of drudgery (Guðrún is married to Atli). Moreover, in both instances the female activists bring about vengeance on their masters.

14/7 *kyrrseta*: this word occurs in Óttarr svarti's *Knútsdrápa* 3 (*Skj* B I, 273) from 1024, but is otherwise a prose word.

14/8 *felli*: the subjunctive implies purpose: the giant girls are actively engaged in toppling Knúi. The construction *áðr . . . felli* is fairly common, however: it occurs in Gísl Illugason's *Erfikvæði* (*c.* 1104) 13/8 (*áðr Hugi felli*: *Skj* B I, 412), and frequently in *Krákumál* (twelfth century) (st. 5, 6, 7, 10, 20: *Skj* B I, 650 ff.). De Vries (1964–7, §129) regards Gísl's phrase as borrowed from *Grottasqngr*, but the expression is too short to draw any firm conclusion.

15/3 *kqppum*: either from *kapp*, 'brave deed', or from *kappi*, 'champion'; cf. *kendir at þegnum*, 'recognised as subordinates' (Óttarr svarti, *Hqfuðlausn* 19, *c.* 1023, *Skj* B I, 272).

15/5 *skorðum . . . geirum*: *skora* (of which *skorðum* is a syncopated preterite), frequent in prose, is found only here in Eddic poetry. Compare Sighvatr's *Erfidrápa* 6/3 (*Skj* B I, 240, *c.* 1040): *hvqssum hundmqrgum [. . .] lét grundar vqrðr með vqpnum skorða víkingum skqr*, 'with sharp weapons the guardian of the land had the heads sheared from a good many Vikings' (though note the *varia lectio* form *skerða*, 'diminish', here; *skorðum* too could be read as *skqrðum*, the preterite of *skerða*). The related *skera* commonly occurs in heroic verse of wounds, in

particular with reference to the cutting out of Hǫgni's heart (*Oddrúnargrátr* 28/5–6, *Atlakviða* 22, 24, *Atlamál* 59, *Guðrúnarhvǫt* 17).
15/8 *brand ruðum*: *rjóða brand* is a fairly frequent expression in skaldic verse (*Skj* B I, 133, 218, 338, 380).

16–17 St. 16 represents the lowest point in the expression of the giantesses' fortunes: in the cold drudgery of slavery these mighty warrior women are forced to turn a mill to produce peace. Menja appears ready to give up milling, but in the next stanza her companion urges her on to grind out not peace but an army of vengeance to overthrow Fróði. A combination of traditions seems to be the poet's purpose here: the peace of frið-Fróði is about to end in the violent overthrow of the murderous Fróði the erstwhile Heathobard.
16/3 *miskunnlausar*: this word does not appear elsewhere in verse. *Miskunn* is found only in late religious verse; the earliest is probably *Harmsól* from the twelfth century (st. 4, 46, *Skj* B I, 549, 560; for further references see *LP*, *s.v.*). A double meaning may be intended in the present context: the obvious sense is '(treated) without pity', but the usual prose sense is 'having no pity (on others)' (see von See et al. 2000, 922–3, for examples). The implication is that the giantesses will also behave without pity in their subsequent treatment of Fróði.
16/5–6 *aurr etr iliar, en ofan kulði*: cf. *Rígsþula* 10/3: *aurr var á ilium*, 'soil was on the soles of her feet', describing Þír, 'Thrall-woman' (see commentary in *PE* II).
16/7 *dólgs siǫtul*: *dólg*, 'enmity, strife', occurs in the most ancient skaldic verse (see *LP* for references); in Eddic poetry it occurs in *Helgakviða Hundingsbana I* 20 (*dólga dynr*, 'din of battle'), and, as in *Grottasǫngr*, in kennings: *dólgrǫgnir*, 'sovereign of enmity' (warrior) (*Atlakviða* 31); *dólgspor*, 'battle trace' (wound) (*Helgakviða Hundingsbana II* 42); *dólgviðr*, 'battle tree' (warrior) (*Sigrdrífumál* 29). *Siǫtull* occurs elsewhere only in a *lausavísa* of Egill (see commentary to 7/3–4), where it means 'seat' (cf. English *settle*); an interpretation of *dólgs siǫtul* as 'seat of enmity' would appear feasible, but instances of 'seat' words being used in the sense of 'source' seem hard to adduce in Old Norse. Whilst lexical influence from Egill's verse is likely, semantically *siǫtul* is better linked here with the derived verb *sjǫtlask*, 'subside, settle', hence *siǫtul* is 'that which settles'. Following the pattern of the heroic and skaldic verse known to him, the poet has formed a striking designation for the mill as a disperser of strife.
16/8 *daprt er at Fróða*: cf. *Hárbarðsljóð* 4/3: *dǫpr ero þín heimkynni*, 'dismal are your home affairs' (Óðinn taunting Þórr). In Eddic poetry the word is found also in *Atlamál* 59/7 (*dag dapran*, 'dismal day'), *Sigurðarkviða in skamma* 54/5 (*daprar miniar*, 'dismal memories'). In all these instances the word is associated with death (respectively a dead mother, the servant's own forthcoming death, a dead husband).

17/4 *of hleyti*: the manuscript form 'leiti' represents a common spelling of *hleyti* in the sense 'share' (Cleasby and Vigfusson 1957, *s.v. hleyti* II). *Of* either means 'over, beyond', hence 'beyond my share', or it is the (chiefly poetic) enclitic particle, of little semantic weight; in noun phrases the word order adjective + *of* + noun, as here, is typical (see Cleasby and Vigfusson 1957, *s.v. of* enclytic particle II); the meaning then would be 'for my part I have milled my share'.

17/5 The change of mood, from Menja's statement that she has milled enough and will stop, to one of defiant refusal to rest the hands before the milling has reached completion, indicates the probability of a change of speaker to Fenja, although there is no indication of this in the manuscripts. The T reading, with the giantesses as subject, is preferable to that of SR with the unclear singular subject (in the subjunctive); there has clearly been confusion of minims in the manuscript tradition.
17/8 The use of the subjunctive *þykki* emphasises the irony: when Fróði's overthrow has been ground out, he will certainly feel enough milling has been performed.

18 Whereas Menja had prophesied riches for Fróði and had finally resigned herself merely to cease milling, Fenja proposes to change the milling to one of hostility, and she prophesies the overthrow of Fróði. He had fallen asleep earlier, dreaming of riches, but is now taunted by Fenja to awake, if he wishes to hear the song they are *now* singing. The *sǫgum fornum* may, as SG argue, refer to the histories the girls have related in st. 9 and following, but the expression carries more weight if it is taken to mean the tales of the feuds and wars Fróði was involved in (such as are alluded to in *Beowulf* when it recounts the history of Froda and Ingeld), ancient to the audience of the poem, though still to happen from the perspective of the characters in the poem; cf. *sǫgom fornom*, 'old tales' (*Oddrúnargrátr* 1/2); *fornom stǫfom*, 'old lore' (*Vafþrúðnismál* 1/5); *fornar rúnar*, 'old runes' (*Vǫluspá* 57/8); *forn spiǫll fira*, 'old news of men [i.e. of the world]' (*Vǫluspá* 1/7); *fornra spialla*, 'old news' (*Helgakviða Hundingsbana I* 36/2).
18/1 *hǫndla*, an emendation of Gudbrand Vigfusson, appears the best solution for this clearly corrupted passage. The SR reading 'hǫlða' ('of freemen') makes at best strained sense ('hands of men shall [become] hard staves'), and presupposes the ellipsis of an infinitive 'be' or 'become'. The T reading 'holda' might readily be taken as standing simply for *halda* (instances of 'o' for 'a' are listed for example in Cleasby and Vigfusson 1957, *s.v. faldr*), but, as von See et al. (2000, 933–4) point out, *halda* in the sense of 'grip' requires a dative. Suspicions are aroused too by the fact that that this is the only place where 'ǫ' occurs in the text of the poem in SR, suggesting innovation by the scribe (such as a misreading of 'ō' as 'ð' and 'correction' to 'ǫ').
18/2 *triónor*: the usual meaning is 'snouts' (*trjónu trolls*, 'snout troll', is found in *Haustlǫng* 17 (*Skj* B I, 18) as a designation of Þórr's hammer). However, von See et al. (2000, 935–6, following SG's earlier suggestion) point out the likely existence of another meaning, 'shaft', found (arguably) in *Eiríks saga rauða* and *Sturlunga*. A meaning 'shaft' and thus 'spear' is clearly called for in *Grottasǫngr*.
18/4–5 The repeated call to awaken, used here as a device to link *helmingar* together (cf. 21/8, 22/1), is reminiscent of *Bjarkamál* 1–2 (*Skj* B I, 171), where a call to awaken as day breaks is made several times: but the call is explicitly to war, not to old stories, as in *Grottasǫngr*. It seems likely that *Grottasǫngr*'s allusion to the older poem underlines the nature of these old songs as ones of war in which Fróði is overthrown.
18/6 The word-order of T is followed as being metrically preferable; even so, the fall of the alliteration on the modal verb *vill* betrays weak poetic technique.

It is possible that the text was corrupted at some point (in which case SR *ef þú hlýða vill* could be correct).
18/8 Cf. *Oddrúnargrátr* 1/2: *í sǫgom fornom*, 'in ancient tales'.

19 The stanza bears a strong resemblance, presumably coincidental, to the Old English *Finnsburh Fragment* lines 3 ff.: *Ne ðis ne dagað eastan, ne her draca ne fleogeð, ne her ðisse healle hornas ne byrnað, ac her forþ berað* [. . .] *nu arisað weadæda* [. . .] *ac onwacnigeað nu, wigend mine, habbað eowre linda*, 'This is not the day dawning from the east, nor is any dragon flying here, nor are the eaves of this hall burning here, but [an army] here brings [weapons] [. . .] now deeds of woe arise [. . .] but awake now, my warriors, hold your shields'. To this may be added the opening of *Bjarkamál*, marking the beginning of battle: *Dagr's upp kominn*, 'Day has arisen'. Behind the 'fire to the east' of *Grottasǫngr* (surely pointing to the dawning day), and the disavowal of the fiery light at Finnsburh being the new day, lies the suspicion that a fiery sky marked the onset of battle: cf. the *vígroði*, 'battle reddening', of *Helgakviða Hundingsbana II* 19. Also to be compared with the scene in *Grottasǫngr* is that described by Saxo (VII, i.7), where Frodo V is attacked and burned in his hall at night, with the implication that he may have been asleep (inferred from his punishment of those that woke him, mentioned previously).
19/1 Cf. *Hyndluljóð* 49/1: *Hyr sék brenna*, 'I see a fire burning'.
19/3 Cf. *Helgakviða Hundingsbana II* 12/8: *vígspiǫll segir*, 'tells news of the battle'. *Vígspiǫll* does not occur elsewhere.
19/4 *viti*: SG take the mention of beacons as evidence for the poem's composition in Norway under Hákon góði (935–61), who made use of warning beacons (*Hákonar saga góða* ch. 22, ÍF 26, 176–7); however, as SG point out, beacons were also used later in Orkney (see *Orkneyinga saga* ch. 69–71). This places the use of such warning beacons in the mid-twelfth century, in both a time and place more likely for the composition of the poem.
19/6 *af bragði*: the expression is common in prose, but occurs sporadically in (fairly late) verse: *Atlamál* 2/7, a *vísa* of *Ragnars saga loðbrókar* (*Skj* B II, 258), and *Krákumál* 25 (*Skj* B I, 655).
19/7 The burning of Fróði in his hall forms the dramatic climax to the revenge taken by the sons of his murdered brother in *Hrólfs saga kraka*; however, in *Skjǫldunga saga* peace-Fróði too is burnt in his hall, by Mýsingr. The poet again has not focused on an event which can be used to distinguish one Fróði from the other.
19/7–8 Neckel (1908, 428) compares the mid-twelfth century Ívarr Ingimundarson's *Sigurðarbǫlkr* 24/7–8 (*Skj* B I, 471): *brunnu byggðir fyr buðlungi*, 'the habitations burnt despite the prince'; this is likely to be borrowed from *Grottasǫngr* (see de Vries 1964–7, §129).
19/8 *buðlungi*: a term for 'prince' derived from Buðli, father of Atli, found, in Eddic poetry, only in heroic poems; it is also used in *Ynglingatal* 32, 34 (*Skj* B I, 13), by Snorri in *Háttatal* 14, 74 (*Skj* B II, 64, 81), and in kennings in skaldic verse (see *LP*, *s.v. buðlungr*).

20/2 Hleiðr was regarded as the ancient seat of the Danish kings; it is identified with the modern hamlet of Lejre, near Roskilde. There may have been some historical basis in this tradition as far as the Danish kings of the fifth to sixth centuries are concerned (including Hrólfr kraki), but Fróði, as a Heathobard originally, would not have lived there. By the time of all the Scandinavian records, Hleiðr is regarded as the seat of all the Fróðis, including peace-Fróði, so little can be concluded from its mention in the poem at this point.

20/3 The T reading *rauðom ringom* is possibly original. Initial *h-* before a consonant is also lacking in T's 'lyða' and 'leiti'. Whilst this would be consistent with a non-Icelandic origin, Icelandic skalds would also have been open to using alliteratively felicitous dialectal variants (the same phrase occurs elsewhere in heroic verse, but often requires *h-*, e.g. at *Þrymskviða* 29).

20/4 *regingrióti*: *regin* normally refers to 'the powers', i.e. the gods, but a basic sense of 'mighty' is more likely here: cf. the *reginþing*, 'mighty assembly', i.e. battle, of *Helgakviða Hundingsbana I* 51. Compare also *reginfjalli*, 'mighty, wild mountain', of *Heiðreks gátur* 10 (*Skj* B II, 242). Possibly a sense of fatality may have adhered to the word *regin*, which is related to Gothic *ragin*, 'judgement', but if he inherited the word *regingriót* with this connotation the poet of *Grottasǫngr* seems not to have been aware of it.

20/4 *mǫndli*: on the 'handle' as a cosmological entity, see the section on 'The cosmic mill' in Introduction V.

20/7 *vamlar*: SR reads 'valmar', where the short line beneath 'lm' indicates that some sort of correction is required; it does not appear to indicate deletion, but may indicate transposition (a similar sign is found elsewhere); possibly the scribe wrote 'val' in anticipation of *valdreyra*. The word *vamall* does not occur in modern Icelandic, but is well recorded elsewhere in Scandinavian languages (e.g. Danish *vammel*, 'sickly'). Another possibility is to follow the T reading 'valnar'; this word too is not found in modern Icelandic, but is well recorded in all other Scandinavian tongues. Particularly apposite is the sense in Norn: *valin*, *valen*, 'benumbed with cold, of limbs, esp. the hands; fumbling, lacking handiness in doing a piece of work' (on this suggestion, see Svavar Sigmundsson 1975). Two orthographic developments are thus possible: *a*. an original 'valnar' was miswritten by the SR scribe as 'valmar' and then corrected with a small line between l and m: the only distraction to cause this miswriting would seem to be the 'ma' in the preceding *eruma*; or *b*. an original 'vamlar' was miswritten in the antecedent of SR and T (which shows clear signs of being a defective text by the time of the writing of SR and T) as 'valmar', under the influence of the several *val-* compounds in the text, in particular of the following *í valdreyra*; this form was copied by the scribe of SR, who marked it as dubious and probably intended a transposition of l and m by his mark, whereas the scribe of T or his antecedent corrected the form to 'valnar'. This implies that the word *valinn* was still understood in Icelandic in the seventeenth century – unless the T scribe was simply interpreting the word as the past participle of *velja*, 'chosen' (for bloodshed, *í valdreyra*) (which would, however, make nonsense of the girls' account of their marching into the fray in many wars, assuming that *eruma* was correctly read as 'we are not').

20/7 *valdreyra* is a highly unusual word, occurring in verse elsewhere only in *Haraldskvæði* 13 (*Skj* B I, 24); the only other comparable compound appears to be *valblóð* (*Guðrúnarhvǫt* 4, *Krákumál* 2 (*Skj* B I, 649)).

21 The reason for the shift to the past tense and to the third person is unclear; the speech appears to be blending with the narrative of lines 5 to 7.
21/1–2 *míns fǫður mær*: for this periphrasis for 'I' cf. *míns fǫður sveinn*, 'my father's boy' (Þórarinn svarti, *Skj* B I, 107), *Sigurðr* [. . .] *mun* [. . .] *mǫgr fǫður kallaðr*, 'Sigurðr will be called son of his father' (*Ragnars saga loðbrókar*, *Skj* B II, 253).
21/7 *iárni varðar*: cf. *Darraðarljóð* 2/7: *járnvarðr yllir*, 'the shed rod is iron-clad'. In the meaningless SR reading 'iarnar fiarþar' the *-ar* of *iarnar* anticipates that of *fiarþar*; 'fi' is doubtless a misreading of an original 'p', the use of which indicates an early manuscript.

22 This stanza is at best corrupt, and probably an interpolation (for a full discussion, see von See et al. 2000, 952–8). The son of Yrsa, called both son and brother, is Hrólfr kraki: Helgi married his own daughter Yrsa unaware of their relationship (*Hrólfs saga kraka* ch. 6; a similar history is related in *Skjǫldunga saga* ch. 11 and Saxo book II). The manuscripts read, in lines 3–4, *við hálfdana hefna Fróða*; this would mean, on the most natural reading, that Hrólfr was taking vengeance *for* Fróði against (though *við* is rarer than *á* in this sense) or alongside the 'half-Danes'. Clearly the vengeance must be taken against Fróði, for which we would expect *á Fróða* (as here emended: the plain dative is, however, possible; see Fritzner 1886–1972 on the various constructions with *hefna*). Half-Danes are nowhere else mentioned in Germanic literature, other than in the Old English *Finnsburh Fragment* (and the associated Episode in *Beowulf* 1069), and the use of the word even there is not clear; Tolkien (1982, 37–45) argues it was rather a 'surname' than a tribal name. The only possible sense in the present context would be 'sons of Hálfdan' (the brother whom Fróði murdered in *Hrólfs saga kraka*). This would indicate that Hrólfr was acting in concert with his father and uncle to take vengeance on Fróði – something with no analogue anywhere in Old Norse literature. Here, the emendation adopted by SG is followed, changing *við* to *vígs*. The form 'halfdana' would have arisen after a scribe had wrongly written *við*, which requires an accusative form, most easily derived from 'halfdanar' by dropping the final -r (even though this changes the sense). However, problems remain: there is no parallel to Hrólfr taking vengeance for his grandfather (an unlikely event in itself); the proposal of SG, that Hrólfr is here regarded as son, not grandson, of Hálfdan is also unparalleled and unlikely. In addition, the second *helmingr* presents us with a very weakly expressed irrelevance scarcely credible as the pinnacle of a curse of vengeance. Moreover, alliteration is weak throughout the stanza: *mon* (2) should be unstressed; in 3 *Hálfdanar vígs* would be better (and *við hálfdana* would again be weak); in 5–6 both *hennar* and *heitinn* are hardly suitable to bear the stress; 8 would be improved as *báðar vitum þat*. As Eiríkr Magnússon points out, the time-frame of the stanza is also out of kilter with the rest of the poem: in 19 the speaker already sees the warning beacon heralding war, yet 22 proclaims a piece of knowledge presumably unknown as yet to the world, that Hrólfr *will* be called both son and brother (and *will* seek vengeance). Such an array of weaknesses in this stanza suggest it is a badly constructed interpolation, based perhaps on a marginal surmise by a previous scribe. Snorri did not know this stanza, or ignored it if he

did, for his tale of Grotti identifies the Fróði as frið-Fróði, not the later brother of Hálfdan; indeed, the poet nowhere else makes such a clear identification, preferring rather to shroud Fróði's identity in a deliberate ambiguity to produce an interplay of characteristics associated, in tradition, with separate characters.

23/2 Cf. *Rígsþula* 9/2: *magns um kosta*, 'to test his might'; *Víkarsbálkr* 16/7–8 (*Skj* B II, 347): *alls megins áðr kostaðek*, 'I had exerted all my strength'.
23/4 *í iǫtunmóði*: in Eddic poetry found elsewhere only in *Vǫluspá* 47/4 (of the world-serpent Jǫrmungandr). It is also found in prose, of giants and trolls.
23/5–8 The *skapttré* is probably a framework above the mill for attaching and steadying the handle (the *skapt*). SG's argument against this, on the ground that *tré* is plural, does not carry much weight: the use of the plural derives from the fact that the apparatus had several parts to it. The manuscript form 'skap' can scarcely be accepted; no sensible meaning for *skap* can be adduced that has any parallels. The *lúðr* would be roughly at waist height; as the great lower stone (*hinn hǫfgi hallr*) fell, it split in two (SG take this to refer here to the upper stone: elsewhere the reference of *hǫfgi hallr* is to the lower stone; the poet is emphasising that even the mighty unmoving base-stone of the quern is shattered).

24/4 The line is suspect: the use of *sem* ('as') appears to be without sense, and the alliterative stress on *munum* is unsatisfactory. It is likely that some lines have been lost before 4.
24/5 *fullstaðit*: this has great ironic value: the girls have stood long enough to accomplish the full circle of fate encompassed by the poem – long enough to fulfil any engagement they have made, long enough to bore and tire them, long enough to grind out all the good and ill that adhered to the name of Fróði.

Bibliography

Eddic poems are edited in *The Poetic Edda*, ed. U. Dronke, vols. I and II (Oxford, 1969, 1997), and in *Kommentar zu den Liedern der Edda*, ed. K. von See et al. (Heidelberg, 1997–). Neither edition is yet complete – texts of other poems may be found in the edition (without commentary) *Edda: die Lieder des Codex Regius*, Text, ed. G. Neckel, rev. H. Kuhn (5th edn, Heidelberg, 1983). A recommended complete translation is *The Poetic Edda*, trans. C. Larrington (Oxford, 1996).

Adam of Bremen, 'Descriptio insularum aquilonis' in *Gesta Hammaburgensis ecclesiae pontificum*, 3rd edn, ed. B. Schmeidler. Scriptores rerum Germanicarum in usum scholarum ex Monumentis Germaniae historicis separatim editi. Hanover and Leipzig, 1917. (Trans. F. J. Tschan, *History of the Archbishops of Hamburg-Bremen*. New York, 2002.)

Ælfric, *De falsis diis*, in *Homilies of Ælfric: A Supplementary Collection*, ed. J. C. Pope. London, 1969.

al-Nadim, Muhammad ibn, 1970. *The Fihrist of Al-Nadim: A Tenth-Century Survey of Muslim Culture*, ed. and trans. B. Dodge. New York and London.

Asbjørnsen, P. C., and J. Moe, 1886. *Norske folke-eventyr*. Christiania.

ATU = Aarne–Thompson–Uther folktale motifs: H.-J. Uther, *The Types of International Folktales: A Classification and Bibliography*, 3 vols. Helsinki, 2004.

Baetke, W., 1942. 'Der Begriff der "Unheiligkeit" im altnordischen Recht', *Beiträge zur Geschichte der deutschen Sprache und Literatur* 66, 1–54.

Bandamanna saga in *Grettis saga Ásmundarsonar, Bandamanna saga*, ed. Guðni Jónsson. Íslenzk fornrit 7, pp. 291–363. Reykjavík, 1936.

Bede, *Ecclesiastical History of the English People*, ed. B. Colgrave and R. A. B. Mynors. Oxford, 1969.

Beowulf: *Klaeber's Beowulf*, ed. R. D. Fulk, R. E. Bjork and J. D. Niles. Toronto. (Trans. S. Heaney, *Beowulf*. London, 1999.)

Bjarni Guðnason, 1963. *Um Skjöldungasögu*. Reykjavík.

Bolte, J., and G. Polívka, 1913–32. *Anmerkungen zu den Kinder- und Hausmärchen der Brüder Grimm*, 5 vols. Leipzig.

Bósa saga in *FSNL* III, pp. 281–322.

Brennecke, D., 1981. 'Gab es eine *Skrýmiskviða*?', *Arkiv för nordisk filologi* 96, 1–8.

Brennu-Njáls saga, ed. Einar Ólafur Sveinsson. Íslenzk fornrit 12. Reykjavík, 1954. (Trans. R. Cook in *The Complete Sagas of Icelanders*, ed. Viðar Hreinsson, 5 vols. Reykjavík, 1997, III 1–222.)

Campbell, J. L, and F. Collinson, 1969–81. *Hebridean Folksongs*, 3 vols. Oxford.

Christiansen, H., 1952. 'Det norrøne ord *lúðr*', *Maal og minne*, 101–6.

Cleasby, R., and G. Vigfusson, 1957. *An Icelandic-English Dictionary*, 2nd edn, rev. W. A. Craigie. Oxford.

Curwen, E. C., 1937. 'Querns', *Antiquity* 11, 133–51.
Danakonunga sǫgur, ed. Bjarni Guðnason. Íslenzk fornrit 35. Reykjavík, 1982.
Darraðarljóð in Poole 1991, 116–56.
Davidson, D. L., 1983. 'Earl Hákon and His Poets'. D.Phil. thesis. Oxford.
Dronke, P. and U., 1998. *Growth of Literature: The Sea and the God of the Sea*. H. M. Chadwick Memorial Lecture 8. Cambridge.
Eiríkr Magnússon, ed., 1910. *Gróttasǫngr*. Coventry.
Faulkes, A., ed., *Edda: Prologue and Gylfaginning*, London, 1988; *Edda: Skáldskaparmál*, 2 vols., London, 1998. (Trans. A. Faulkes, *Edda*, London, 1987.)
Finnsburh Fragment in *Beowulf* (ed. Klaeber).
First Grammatical Treatise, 2nd edn, ed. E. Haugen. London, 1972.
Flateyjarbók, ed. Sigurður Nordal et al., 4 vols. Akranes, 1944–5.
Fritzner, J., 1886–1972. *Ordbog over det gamle norske sprog*, 3 vols + supplementary 4th vol. Kristiania (Oslo).
FSNL = *Fornaldar sögur norðurlanda*, ed. Guðni Jónsson, 4 vols. Reykjavík, 1954.
Fulk, R. D., 1989. 'An Eddic Analogue to the Scyld Scefing Story', *Review of English Studies* 40, 313–22.
Gollancz, I., 1898. *Hamlet in Iceland*. London.
Hamel, A. G. van, 1934. 'The Game of the Gods', *Arkiv för nordisk filologi* 50, 218–42.
Haraldssona saga in *Heimskringla* III.
Harva, U., 1943. *Sammon ryöstö*. Porvoo.
Heimskringla, ed. Bjarni Aðalbjarnarson, 3 vols. Íslenzk fornrit 26–8. Reykjavík, 1941–51.
Hjálmþérs saga ok Ǫlvers in *FSNL* IV, pp. 177–243.
Holmberg, U., 1922–3. *Der Baum des Lebens*. Helsinki.
Holtsmark, A., 1946. 'Det norrøne ord *lúðr*', *Maal og minne*, 49–65.
Hrólfs saga kraka in *FSNL* I, pp. 1–105.
Hrólfs saga kraka, ed. D. Slay. Copenhagen, 1960.
ÍF = Íslenzk fornrit, published by Hið íslenzka fornritafélag, Reykjavík.
JH = Jón Helgason, *Eddadigte*, 3 vols. Copenhagen, 1951.
Johnston, A., 1908–9. 'Grotta söngr and the Orkney and Shetland Quern', *Saga-Book* 6, 296–304.
Jón Árnason 1863–4. *Íslenzkar þjóðsögur og æfintýri*, 2 vols. Leipzig.
KLNM = *Kulturhistorisk leksikon for nordisk middelalder*, 22 vols. Copenhagen, 1956–78.
Kock, E. A., 1923–35. *Notationes Norrœnæ: Anteckningar till Edda och skaldediktning*. Lund.
Koivulehto, J., 1999. 'Varhaiset indoeurooppalaiskontaktit: aika ja paikka lainasanojen valossa', in *Pohjan poluilla: suomalaisten juuret nykytutkimuksen mukaan*, ed. P. Fogelberg. Helsinki, pp. 207–36.
Krappe, A. H., 1924. 'The Song of Grotti', *The Modern Language Review* 19:3, 325–34.
—— 1936. 'Apollon Σμινθεύς and the Teutonic Mýsing', *Archiv für Religionswissenschaft* 33, 40–56.
Kuusi, M., 1949. *Sampo-Eepos: Typologinen analyysi*. Suomalais-Ugrilaisen Seuran Toimituksia 96. Helsinki.
Kuusi, M., K. Bosley and M. Branch, ed. and trans., 1977. *Finnish Folk Poetry: Epic*. Helsinki.

Kålund, K., 1908–18. *Alfræði íslenzk*, 3 vols. Samfund til udgivelse af gammel nordisk litteratur 37, 41, 45. Copenhagen.

Landnámabók, ed. Jakob Benediktsson. Íslenzk fornrit 1. Reykjavík, 1968. (Trans. Hermann Pálsson and P. Edwards, *The Book of Settlements*, Winnipeg, 1972.)

LP = Sveinbjörn Egilsson, *Lexicon poëticum antiquae linguae septentrionalis*, 2nd edn, ed. Finnur Jónsson. Copenhagen, 1931.

Lid, N., 1949. 'Kalevalan Pohjola', *Kalevalan seuran vuosikirja* 29, 104–20.

Lönnrot, E., 1958. *Suomalais-ruotsalainen sanakirja, Finskt-svenskt lexicon*, 3rd edn, 2 vols. Helsinki (repr. of 1874–80 edn).

Mabinogion, trans. J. Gantz. Harmondsworth, 1976.

McKinnell, J., 2005. *Meeting the Other in Norse Myth and Legend*. Cambridge.

McKinnell, J., R. Simek and K. Düwel 2004. *Runes, Magic and Religion: A Sourcebook*. Vienna.

Neckel, G., 1908. *Beiträge zur Eddaforschung*. Dortmund.

Njáls saga = *Brennu-Njáls saga*.

Nordal, Guðrún, 2001. *Tools of Literacy: The Role of Skaldic Verse in Icelandic Textual Culture of the Twelfth and Thirteenth Centuries*. Toronto, Buffalo and London.

Noreen, A., 1970. *Altnordische Grammatik I: Altisländische und altnorwegische Grammatik*, 5th edn. Tübingen.

North, R., 1997. *Heathen Gods in Old English Literature*. Cambridge.

O'Flaherty, W., 1975. *Hindu Myths*. Harmondsworth.

Óláfs saga Tryggvasonar in *Flateyjarbók*.

Olsen, M., 1941–60. *Norges innskrifter med de yngre runer*, 5 vols. (with subsequent volumes by other editors). Oslo.

Orkneyinga saga, ed. Finnbogi Guðmundsson. Íslenzk fornrit 34. Reykjavík, 1965. (Trans. Hermann Pálsson and P. Edwards. London, 1978.)

Ovid, *Metamorphoses I–VIII*, trans. F. J. Miller, rev. G. P. Goold, 3rd edn. Loeb Classical Library. Cambridge, Mass., and London, 1977.

Paris Psalter in *The Paris Psalter and the Meters of Boethius*, ed. G. P. Krapp. Anglo-Saxon Poetic Records V. New York and London, 1932.

PE I = *The Poetic Edda, volume I: Heroic Poems*, ed. U. Dronke. Oxford, 1969.

PE II = *The Poetic Edda, volume II: Mythological Poems*, ed. U. Dronke. Oxford, 1997.

Poole, R. G., 1991. *Viking Poems on War and Peace: A Study in Skaldic Narrative*. Toronto Medieval Texts and Translations 8. Toronto.

Ragnars saga loðbrókar in *FSNL* I, pp. 219–85.

Rímnasafn, ed. Finnur Jónsson, 2 vols. Copenhagen, 1905–22.

Rune Poem, in *The Anglo-Saxon Minor Poems*, ed. E. V. K. Dobbie. Anglo-Saxon Poetic Records VI. New York, 1942.

Rymbegla Collection in Kålund 1908–18, II.

Saxo Grammaticus, *Gesta Danorum*, ed. J. Olrik and H. Ræder, 2 vols. Copenhagen, 1931–57. (Trans. P. Fisher and H. Ellis Davidson, 2 vols. Cambridge, 1979–80.)

Schier, K., 1968. 'Freys und Fróðis Bestattung', in *Festschrift für O. Höfler zum 65. Geburtstag*, ed. H. Birkan and O. Gschwantler. Vienna, pp. 389–409.

See, K. von, 1981. 'Der Germane als Barbare', *Jahrbuch für internationale Germanistik* 13, 42–72.

See, K. von, B. La Farge, E. Picard and K. Schulz 2000. *Kommentar zu den Liedern der Edda*, III: *Götterlieder*. Heidelberg.

Setälä, E. N., 1932. *Sammon arvoitus*. Helsinki.

SG = B. Sijmons and H. Gering, eds, *Die Lieder der Edda*, 3 vols. Halle, 1888–1931.

Simek, R., 1993. *A Dictionary of Northern Mythology*. Cambridge.

Simek, R., and Hermann Pálsson 1987. *Lexikon der altnordischen Literatur.* Stuttgart.

Skj = *Den norsk-islandske skjaldedigtning*, ed. Finnur Jónsson, 4 vols. Copenhagen, 1912–15.

Skjǫldunga saga in *Danakonunga sǫgur*, 1–90.

SnE = Snorri Sturluson, *Edda*, ed. Finnur Jónsson. Reykjavík, 1931.

Stockholm Homily Book: *Homilíu-bók*, ed. T. Wisén. Lund, 1872.

Suomen kansan vanhat runot [Ancient poems of the Finnish people] are available online at http://www.finlit.fi/skvr/

Svavar Sigmundsson 1975. 'Eitt orð í Grottasöng', *Opuscula* 5, 237–40.

Sven Aggesen, *Brevis historia regum Dacie*, in *Scriptores minores historiae Danicae*, vol. I, ed. M. C. Gertz. Copenhagen, 1970 [1917–18], pp. 94–141. (Trans. in Eric Christiansen, *The Works of Sven Aggesen*. London, 1992, 48–74.)

Tacitus, Cornelius, *Germania*, in *Opera minora*, ed. M. Winterbottom and R. M. Ogilvie, Oxford, 1975. (Trans. J. B. Rives. Oxford, 1999.)

Tolkien, J. R. R., ed., 1982. *Finn and Hengest: The Fragment and the Episode*, ed. A. Bliss (posthumously). London.

Tolley, C., 1994–5. 'The Mill in Norse and Finnish Mythology', *Saga-Book* 24, 63–82.

—— 1996. 'Beowulf's Scyld Scefing Episode: Some Norse and Finnish Analogues', *Arv* 52, 7–48.

Upphaf allra frásagna in *Danakonunga sǫgur*, 39–40.

Vries, J. de, 1956–7. *Altgermanische Religionsgeschichte*, 2nd edn, 2 vols. Berlin.

—— 1964–7. *Altnordische Literaturgeschichte*, 2nd edn, 2 vols. Berlin.

—— 1977. *Altnordisches etymologisches Wörterbuch*, 3rd edn. Leiden.

Watts, V. E., 2004. *The Cambridge Dictionary of English Place-Names*. Cambridge.

Weber, G., 1970. 'Die Christus-Strophe des Eilífr Goðrúnarson', *Zeitschrift für deutsches Altertum und deutsche Literatur* 99, 87–90.

Widsith: A Study in Old English Heroic Legend, ed. R. W. Chambers. Cambridge, 1912.

Wyatt, N., 1998. *Religious Texts from Ugarit: The Words of Ilimilku and His Colleagues*. Sheffield.

Ynglinga saga in *Heimskringla* I, 1–83.

Ynglingatal is included within *Ynglinga saga*.

Ǫgmundar þáttr dytts in *Eyfirðinga sǫgur*, ed. Jónas Kristjánsson. Íslenzk fornrit 9, pp. 99–115. Reykjavík, 1956. (Trans. J. McKinnell in *The Complete Sagas of Icelanders*, ed. Viðar Hreinsson, 5 vols. Reykjavík, 1997, II 314–22. The Flateyjarbók version is edited in I. Wyatt, *Two Tales of Icelanders*. Durham, 1993, 1–9.)

Ǫlkofra þáttr in *Austfirðinga sǫgur*, ed. Jón Jóhannesson. Íslenzk fornrit 11, pp. 83–94. Reykjavík, 1950.

Ǫrvar-Odds saga in *FSNL* II, pp. 199–363. (Trans. Hermann Pálsson and P. Edwards, *Arrow-Odd. A Medieval Novel*. London, 1970.)